To Join the Lost

Book One of In Dante's Wake

Seth Steinzor

Fomite
Burlington, VT

Poems copyright 2016 © by Seth Steinzor

All rights reserved. No part of this book may be reproduced in any form or by any means without the prior written consent of the publisher, except in the case of brief quotations used in reviews and certain other noncommercial uses permitted by copyright law.

ISBN-13: 978-1-942515-64-7
Library of Congress Control Number: 2016953062

Fomite
58 Peru Street
Burlington, VT 05401
www.fomitepress.com

Cover Art Jennifer Gammon
To see more of Jennifer's art,
visit https://squareup.com/store/jennifergammonart/

Acknowledgments

Thanks to Sam Fishman, my maternal grandfather, that forceful, courageous, exasperating man, whose boxes of essays chaotically typed on erratically collated onionskin demonstrated for me that a writer is someone who writes, period, and if anybody else reads it that's very nice but the practice is no less honorable if they don't (an important lesson for a poet!); to Joan Kassman Price, whose teaching of literature at St. Michael's Epsicopalian Country Day School in Florence, Italy, was not the least of the marvels of that marvelous year 1967-1968: her dream that she was reading a book of poems by me entitled "Stories" is something I have tried to live up to ever since; to Vicky Carter, RIP; to Robert Rossel, Ph.D; to Susan Weiss, RIP, for providing the venue where many of these cantos first were tried out on the public; to Marc Estrin, for his generous approbation; and to Rennie McQuilkin, for well, what can I say? — being the editor one would dream of working with, if one knew how good working with an editor could be.

In Dante's Wake is dedicated to Ben and Ida

Contents

Canto I	1
Canto II	8
Canto III	13
Canto IV	19
Canto V	27
Canto VI	33
Canto VII	39
Canto VIII	44
Canto IX	51
Canto X	59
Canto XI	65
Canto XII	71
Canto XIII	79
Canto XIV	86
Canto XV	94
Canto XVI	100
Canto XVII	106
Canto XVIII	113
Canto XIX	119
Canto XX	125
Canto XXI	132
Canto XXII	138
Canto XXIII	145
Canto XXIV	152
Canto XXV	159
Canto XXVI	167
Canto XXVII	174

Canto XXVIII	181
Canto XXIX	187
Canto XXX	194
Canto XXXI	200
Canto XXXII	208
Canto XXXIII	214
Canto XXXIV	221
Afterword	231

Canto I

Midway through my life's journey, I found myself
lost in a dark place, a tangle of hanging
vines or cables or branches – so dark! – festooning
larger solid looming walls or
trunks or rocks or rubble, and strange shapes
moving through the mist, silent or
howling, scuffling through the uneven dirt or
dropping from the blotchy sky like
thicker clouds, so close sometimes I ducked in
fright so that they never quite touched me.

Someone I had trusted had led me there.
Perhaps it was persons, I could not remember,
only how their words and gestures, once so
sensible and clear, gradually grew
obscure, how their features, once so individual
and expressive – this lifted tuft of
eyebrow, that kindly smile, that belly laugh –
smoothed to nothing in the murk,
and how at last they turned away, gibbering,
gone. Without them was no path

that I could see. A bit ahead to the right the
curtain seemed lighter, its patterns more
distinct and loosely entwined and permeable,
so I stepped over that way, stumbling
on the occasional root or protuberance,
until I splashed ankle deep
into a pool of sucking mud that spread
among the blackened boles and mounds its
unforgiving mirror far as could be
seen, and I could go no farther.

Perhaps, I thought, what I had followed, moth-like,
was just the sky's dim luminescence
the marsh cast back, and then I knew despair,
and pulled my sodden shoe back out, and
turned, and a cry swelled in my throat. But just
before I let it loose, another
shimmer caught my eye. Perhaps, I thought,
I'd wandered off my course through tending
to my feet and not to where they were going;
and holding my gaze level, and gingerly

feeling the way with toes that slid forward and sometimes
up and around or suddenly down (so
my attention was sharply bifurcated
while a third, unattended
part of me coordinated) towards that
distant barely backlit scrim, while
yet a fourth part of my poor divided

self was straining not to feel a
thing at all. Of all four tasks, this last was
hardest. Hope and fear impelled me

"Run!" but who could run on that turf, rough and
sharp as a grater? And vehement voices
muttering a flow of words so soft they'd
lost their forms now clogged my hearing,
aural mush, except that here and there, as
clear and hard as pebbles, numbers
struck me; and unseen hands behind me plucked my
clothing, grabbed my shoulders, stroked my
hair. My knees gave way. I huddled there, in
sudden lonely silence, long.

Then slowly, like a fern uncurling, I rose,
not recalling having fallen
asleep or having passed the border into
awareness of this dismal dawn.
Before me, jarringly stood the only straight
and undistorted object in my
view: a man, tall and thin, head topped by
what I took to be a red fleece
ski hat, barefoot, robed in simple brown he'd
cinched about the waist with a cord.

His skinny neck, that sprouted from an itchy
looking undergarment, upheld
a long and narrow face. A long and narrow

nose, sharply hooked, ran like a
ridge between the hills of his high cheekbones,
and the basins of his cheeks
converged upon a small and beautiful mouth.
The upper lip was thin and long,
the lower shorter, plusher, so the top one
drooped a little at the corners,

and they made an arc much like a bow
whose arrows aim to pierce the clouds,
not quite primly frowning, more the meeting of
strength and sensitivity. But his
great, sad, brown eyes! There's a
distant gaze that looks within,
and a regard like a net we cast upon the
outer world, that in his eyes were
combined: alertly pensive, missing nothing.
They were what held me. I stepped forward.

Glancing at my squelching shoes, "*O voi che
siete in piccioletta barca,*"
he said, "Oh you who follow me in
little boats." His voice was sweet and
soft, and the phrase was one of the few I knew in
Italian. Odder to meet an Italian who
can't quote Dante than one who can. Well!
Humor was the last thing I'd
expected in that desolation. Taken
quite aback, I paused, and at that

instant, growls, a vicious snarl, a rumble
low and ominous, all issued
from behind the stumps of a shattered pylon
thirty feet away. His robe
flaring, he whirled and faced the hidden beasts.
"Whatever you were seeking, you won't
find it here," he said, glancing back.
(Oddest: how I did not find it
odd to understand him.) "If you don't lose your
way yourself, those three will lose it

for you. Come, and I will show you the path
out of here." And backing slowly
towards me over shards and ankle-busting
holes as if his feet had eyes,
he glided, holding all the while the animal
danger at bay by looking at it with
fiercer focus than any predator, then
guided me some yards away
behind a ragged rubbish berm. I thought he'd
stop to talk, then. Instead, assured

I was still with him and unharmed, he whirled so his
garment flared like a tulip again, and
strode away, impatiently gesturing at me
to follow. Not that I had much choice,
but still I hesitated. Then I gathered
up my hope and hurried after,

catching up with him a while before I
caught my breath enough to ask him,
"Who are you? And what do you want with me?"
He answered: "Last things first. You are

the one whose fifteenth year blossomed in the
city by the Arno, where they were
drying the pages of books the river had drenched
two years before?" My face froze. He nodded.
"And of course you've not forgotten her
you stood with by the river wall,
your arms around each other's waists, not holding,
sweetly ratifying the seal your
bodies made from ankle to shoulder?" I could not
move. He halted with me. "And how

you stood there, watched the brown-green flood,
minute by minute on the brink of a kiss
that never came because you were afraid?
Well, it was she who visited me
from one of those bright circles you cannot
quite bring yourself to believe in, glowing
and slender and blonde and passionate, and she asked me
to help you find your way. She called you
My Seth, whom I knew as a poet and one of love's authors.
She knew how to ask so her will would be mine."

With finely calculated disregard
for how much shock I could absorb,

he added, "As for who I am: that year
you met and said good-bye to her
not knowing how long, you lived in my home town,
the place they kicked me out of and
set death at the gate to keep me away. You lived
in a small hotel off Via Fiume
named for her whose hand reached down for me
as your Victoria reaches for you."

Canto II

Hearing him speak of her, heat flooded me,
filled me like water in a vessel
trembling just above the brim; his riddle,
who he was, breezed by my ears
just barely heard; but like a breath that ruffles
first, then breaks the surface tension
so that something overflows, it stirred me
to turn and stride as briskly as the
ground allowed along the head-high ridge
the way we had been going. He followed

quietly, allowing me to escape
among my memories. This was
not the first time strangeness had engulfed me.
When Vicky was sixteen, her death
obliterated all the geography
dividing the East coast from the West.
That summer, an eighteen year old with perfect breasts
introduced me to man's reverse
passage up the birth canal, expanding
the bounds of her waiting boyfriend's feelings,

*or so they said. It consummated something
that Vicky had rendered irrelevant, almost.
After, the three of us ate spaghetti together.
That summer, full of tear gas and protests,
I had a part time job at a Buffalo diner,
busing tables and washing dishes,
dumping the ketchup-sodden fries and lumps of
meat, wilted lettuce, tomato
slices, random peas and mashed with gravy
into battered, waist-high bins, then*

*loading racks and shoving them along a
track of stainless steel into a
box of stainless steel – lower the lever,
close the gate – punch the big red
button, wait – shuddering, hissing – raise
the gate, releasing white clouds –
reach in, extract a rack of formerly filthy,
now gleaming and steaming glasses, or shiny,
clunky porcelain, or scratched-up aluminum
knives, forks, and spoons so hot*

*you couldn't touch them. Amy, the waitress/manager,
used to call me towards shift's end
to "do the garbage." Behind the counter was hidden
the barrel where they dumped the napkins,
smeary placemats, newspapers, coffee filters,
wet brown mounds of grounds, tea bags,
sugar packets, little plastic jelly*

*cuplets scraped mostly clean. I jumped
right in and stomped around like making wine,
transforming full to half empty.*

*No need now to haul it to the malodorous bins
out back and hoist and heave it
in among the flies and yellow jackets.
"You crazy kid," said Amy, pleased.
I lowered my hands to the barrel's rounded rim,
and balanced a moment on my straightened
arms surveying the place – devoid of any but
waitresses awaiting the dinner rush, their
faces relaxed, two smiling and sharing a smoke,
all self-contained, about to be*

*awash in the stream of eaters. By then I'd be gone.
So I folded a leg and swung it
over, and the other, and, unsteady – a
sailor newly arrived on land –
retreated to my bright-lit, private space
of steam and water. Withdrew from my pocket
a pill. Unwrapped the foil – hesitated –
tossed it past my back teeth – gulped.
Pulled on my jacket and clocked out, greeting
cadaverous fortyish Juan, my relief.*

*Fortyish. By then, I'd be gone. We never spoke,
except for social noises. But stranger
to me than Juan was what found me outside.*

Intersecting streets, a puddle
wrapped around the curb, the rain so lazy
I counted seconds between the pocks.
The streetlight's reflection ceases shivering before
the next drop falls. Its undulation
slows to a motionless glare, bathed in black.
Coiling around it, purple, green,

so subtle at first I didn't see them, violet
tendrils, loops, curlicues, dashed and
dotted by pomegranate-seed-sized raindrops,
colors exuded from the road's
cold tar, exhausted oils of passing cars,
flickering like the fires in opals.
How long I stood there staring, I don't know.
So thin the slicks, so depthless this
quotidian aurora! Invisible depths
beneath the surface it floated on!

Incommensurables! Whacked ajar by the drug,
my mind encompassed them, and stalled.
Stride through the puddle?! I'd just as soon step out of an
airplane onto a cloud. I mustered
my grit and stretched a shaky leg across.
Just then, my guide's voice recalled me
to the here and now. "There. That is
where we're going." Tiny with distance,
a gate's dark posts and struts, and letters sour
cherry red atop it; below it,

on the ground, I saw a smudge, as if
some sort of shadow. That didn't seem right.
Then something obscured it, quick as a passing thought,
amorphous, shifting, granulated.
So flocks of passenger pigeons hid the sun,
a hundred years ago, until
the milliners cleared the sky. I turned, accepting
the situation's logic, to ask him
what and why and how, and met his steady
gaze and sadly loving smile.

Canto III

"All in due time," he said. "For now, just walk
the way that we were going. Ahead."
Our eyes locked. His showed mine no more than his
command. Mine wavered. So, we walked.
The blazing letters, haloed with haze, grouped into
almost-legible words, were only
intermittently visible, just as,
looking in winter across a valley at
evening milking time, the lights of a barn on the
opposite hillside wink through squalls.

"If, in some sense, you are who you say
you are, well, this is not what I,
or Gustav Doré, for that matter, pictured
from your book," I called to him.
"Yes, that puzzles you," he disappointingly
replied. "Consider the relation
between a word and all it represents.
And watch your step." As we approached,
our pace disjointed by hummocks of refuse – shell casings,
wrappers from military rations,

punctured tires, coils of razor wire,
plastic bags and candy wrappers and
cereal boxes and unidentifiable
bits of organic matter, concrete in
various degrees of structural integrity,
dead trees, car parts, used condoms, rags –
I glanced up from my feet to catch my bearings
and when I registered what I saw,
I stopped on the spot. Almost overhead,
a flock flapped silently, countless life-size

human silhouettes, translucent and thin as if
cut from plastic food wrap, shitting
shredded newsprint that covered and softened the uneven
contours below, steady as snow and
almost as white. "These are the miserable many,"
my guide, now standing beside me, instructed,
"who lived for neither good nor ill. Voiceless,
having squandered that great gift of
naming, praising, cursing – perhaps they'd like to
scream their frustration, loose their envy of

all those not condemned to eternal boredom,
but none can do here what he did not
do where you'll be returning. When first I saw
this place, my leader hurried me on.
But you, who do not know what to believe –
look your fill, in case you see
something you're willing to recognize." I heard

contempt; and shame and anger hardened my
gaze until I barely could see. But something
flickered on the fluttering figure

above me, and what I'd felt at what I'd heard was
driven aside by what I saw.
Peel a cloudy day's dapple off a stream,
hang this sheen in the air, and watch
its pulse and flow form fluid human features,
and each of its fellows alike: a static
crowd of moving parts that, overlapping,
layer almost to opacity,
the eye drawn in, each figure a mottled window
into unimaginable

dimensions, an almost empty pane. I heard
my voice say, "It was not contempt,"
and his, so gently, "For you? No, never, my son,"
and my eyes grew wet and blurry.
He turned to the flock and opened wide his arms
and called, "Come, my friends, let's talk
of poems and what is in them," and they scattered
the way that birds at a feeder flee
when a face appears at the window, clearing
our way to the horrible gate.

Then something in me broke and let me take him
for what he was. Embarrassed, I stooped,
picked up a handful of shreds, and read, "Bennifer,"

and names of sports teams, and "Robert
McNamara," who withheld his truth.
I showed this last to Dante. He said,
"His name is here, his body above. He's struggled
hard to trade his place among these
starvelings for one in purgatory.
He doesn't know the law that if you

have your cake you've got to eat it, too."
Without explaining this cryptic remark,
he strode past the curtain of cling film people, and I
had to hurry to follow. I still could hear
them rustling behind me when we paused before
the awful gate. Its overarching
slogan's sullen fire quivered the air.
My eyes, however, fixed beneath on the
ruin that I had thought from afar was a shadow.
But now I read the tortured iron:

PER ME SI VA NE LA CITTÀ DOLENTE, PER ME
SI VA NE L'ETTERNO DOLORE, PER ME
SI VA LA PERDUTA GENTE. GIUSTIZIA MOSSE…
the rest, just fragments I could not read.
"Some say that Nietzche broke that, coming through,
but I think he had help," my guide
offered. Then, he answered my unasked question.
"For saying *when you go to women,
bring a whip.* And other things. He's learned
that god need not be dead for all

to be permitted, and yet, though all may be
permitted, yes, there is a hell."
He gestured up. "But here, where all is lost,
the more it changes the more it's the same.
Regard with pride your century's contribution."
And through the quaking air, which should have
roared with the heat of those words, but instead quite meekly
bore away faint streaks of black
as if the dust it carried were burned to soot,
my stinging eyes took in the bloody

gothic phrase: ARBEIT MACHT FREI.
"You speak of god," I said. "I tell you,
I am no believer." I struggled then,
my words cast down in my throat by doubt
and fear. Unhesitatingly, he read me.
"Here is the city unforgiven,
believe it. And here am I to show you through.
Believe that, too. Who needs your faith?
Not me. Not your Victoria. Not the fate
that circles your motionless feet like a hawk

that sees a rabbit. Will you let its talons grab you,
paralyzed for fear of looking
behind a three-letter word? What do you think
lurks there? Could it be any worse than the
wasteland where we found each other?" Approaching
the gate on our side was a narrow

platform, long as a subway train, on which
my eyes rested while what he said
beat upon and slowly tore some inner
membrane. There I saw, so faintly

at first but, as that barrier grew more porous,
as if my life and the surrounding death
osmotically were reaching equilibrium,
ever clearer and seemingly solid
shades like bodies striding off the local,
more and more, commuters at rush hour,
hitting the pavement and heading for the rubicund
exit, hardly aware the sign
had changed from "Harvard Square" or "54th Street,"
and though I knew that death had undone

so many – well, it's one thing to count, another
to stand on a beach and feel the sand
shifting deeper about one's ankles. So
I nodded to my patient guide and,
once he came beside me, holding close
to him as a child to its father, I joined
the shuffling throng, through the baleful arch and
down a littered slope, towards a
river, and a boat slip, and a white-maned
man gesticulating wildly.

Canto IV

The ground was rough. The slope went gently down.
I trudged – he seemed to glide – beside
the stream of commuters. I mostly attended to
my feet so as not to tred on something
foul, but my choice of what should be avoided
narrowed the filthier my sneakers became.
With each new besmirchment, I was more free
to look ahead and around. At last
my glances lengthened into observations.
I watched the multitudes, their eyes

downcast, sink as smoothly as if they were riding
an escalator into a dark,
rectangular patch on the ground that wavered
like a black and white movie projected
through smoke onto a dirty sheet, and there
they disappeared. "That is a tunnel.
It takes them under the river, there being too many
bound for hell from your sweet century
for Charon and his boat to ferry as they
did in my day." So my guide.

"But you would not strain through. For you – well, wait.
I'll talk to the boatman. He carried me once,
when I was in the flesh." Descending to the
channel, the slope became steeper, the footing
more slippery. Carefully planting each step, I recalled
my leader's report of the crimson lightning,
the thunder, the quaking earth he'd fainted at
right here. He'd revived across
the river not knowing how he'd crossed it. So I
might see what he had missed! I cloaked my

excitement with deferential tones: "If I
remember right, from your description,
the wintry-haired gent with blazing eyes is Charon.
But who's that in the white coat standing
next to him?" Erect and debonair,
gracefully gesturing towards us as if to
point us out to his wild companion, whose sunset
gaze already glared on us.
"A newcomer. I don't know. Beware of him."
His sudden curtness seemed reproachful.

I wondered if he, no longer confined to a skull,
might know my thoughts as well as I did.
Before I could form the question, he wandered off
with Charon, leaving me to the charming
company of Charon's handsome sidekick,
who offered no greeting but told me the boat
was reserved for those who found distasteful the tunnel's

"promiscuous commingling." On those
worn benches not long ago Strom Thurmond
sat face to face with Idi Amin

on his spread lap, pressing knees with Adolf H. whose
nose was buried in the groin of
Rabbi Meir Kahane and vice versa –
"sixty-nine... efficiently
we bundle them in." He swept an elegant arm at the
empty dinghy – "I give you... our yacht!" –
and wound the other around my shoulders, a friendly
hug. At Dante's yell I pulled
away, too late. The hand clapped to my face a
wad of white wet cotton, a sharpsweet reek.

"You'd like to know what happened," stated my guide,
just as my waking eyes beheld
the boat at its dock now on the far side of the
guck that lapped the pebbles by my
cheek. The boat's attendants grabbed some wretch's
arms and neck and shoved him in.
Combined with my headache, that sight shut my eyes.
So I lay there, not talking, until I could
sit, my nausea slowly abating, breathing
through my mouth to avoid the river's

stinks, until they seemed to coat my tongue;
then I used my nose for as long as
I could stand it. "Old Charon said his friend's a

doctor who volunteered for here while
still above the ground and there showed his fitness.
He helps him subdue unruly passengers.
Being escorted, you seemed such a one. He was
much intrigued by the state of your lungs, and
wished to keep you for study until reminded of
all the other demands on his time."

I gasped at the thought, then retched. He heard, and went on,
"I have been thinking of lines you wrote:
We are pusillanimous in the face of
ghosts and *we, in whose days corpses are*
bulldozed to mass graves and not allowed to
linger for farewells at home.
You live in a sadly mangled place, brother,
that cuts itself off from the presence of death.
You hide the corpses and hunger for the power
your brutal imaginations give them.

You fear that what your lives so busily miss
will be forced upon you – absolute
repose and indifference. You abhor vacuums.
Behind your head is a shadowy bag
you stuff with every threat and terror. Dragging
that, how can you be fully alive,
no matter how your bodies ooze with health?"
I hoped he wasn't expecting an answer.
I kept my mouth shut for a long while as we
picked our way, step by step, through the

          bleary dimness beneath a heavy sky.
        I blush to recall the hope he'd inflamed,
      that soon, the great pagan poets would welcome me
            as they had him, at least as a colleague
        if not as a peer. We climbed the bank and then
              resumed the long descent. He led me
       with such care that I suffered more from my
           impatience than from stumbling, though I
         did that, too. At long, long last, the distance
              was made visible by a dome-shaped

  brightness almost diurnal we seemed to approach
           forever; and there, my hope was dashed,
            as hope must be in that place. It was flat,
             and green, enormous, like playing fields
        floodlit at twilight, and empty. A cyclone fence
                 surrounded it, in places leaning
          to the ground, nowhere straight, its rusty
                gates awry on broken hinges.
        Far away, a figure dressed in black, whose
                singularity starkened how

         the place's vastness yawned untenanted,
                stood by a leaning lightpole,
   but as we grew closer and Dante yelled, "Hey, you!"
          he hurried off into the dark like someone
         eager not to be caught in a just finished act.
             "Where are all the souls you wrote

you saw here – the virtuous pagans?" I asked, and moved
by something weak and liquid, added,
"father?" "Flown," he said, "released by your
'uncertain disbelief,' I'll call it,

from the suspense in which my certainties hung them.
Like the molecule of air that
Julius Caesar exhaled into your mouth
they hover, giving you CPR."
On the lamppost, taped there perhaps by the one who'd
just escaped us, a yellow handbill
covered some older, tattered ones. Cheaply
printed in black and white, like the xeroxed
notices a high school rock band litters
around the neighborhood that sustains

and contains its dreams of glory, crudely lettered,
it read, "CHARLES BAUDELAIRE and Friends
Reading Tonight at Café After Hours
five drink minimum no cover
open mike after last call DOOR PRIZE
Be There Or Be Square." "Oh. damn!"
said Dante, "I had wanted to go to that.
I hear that Virgil might be there.
It's always the same few faces, and sometimes he shows.
Oh, well...next time. Look! There's another!

That one comes here often, says it reminds him
of his beloved Dublin, and he

likes the swimming." "I can see no water."
"No but he can. Jimmy Joyce,
Vieni qui! C'e qualcun' chi vuol' si conosce!"
And when the weedy moustached shade
approached, he peered at me and asked,
"Maestro, should I know him?" "No, but he,
not knowing that you read yourself alone,
was hoping that some day you will

count him as one who seeks to write of people
as if they were human beings. Now,
my son, don't be shy. Speak your mind."
And I: "Forgive – " And he: "Excuse
my curiosity," and leaning, peering
closer, "do I see you breathe?"
"Well, yes," I said. And he to Dante: "May you be
luckier in your followers
than I have been in mine, a bunch of idolatrous
stylesnatching gaseous vacant *ism*ists!"

"If he attends, he may do both of us credit.
Come on, my boy, don't take all day!"
And I, at last: "Not all of us confuse
your words with what is living in them.
You take my meaning." And then I stammered a bit,
and blurted, "Where are all the others?
The virtuous pagans? Homer, Virgil, Whitman,
Blake, and Yeats, and Williams, and Pound?"
"Ah, the place evolves, don't it? Beyond the

power of our invention, no less

changed by us, much like that place where you and
I will never coincide.
Mais, plus ça change... they never really missed that
hope our boyo here denied them, so
now they're gone for good from this oasis
except for visits for bowling matches,
amiable ambles, the spiritual slap and tickle,
it's all the same to them. Well, Pound...
of those you named, he rode the boat that you did,
but he had Mengele's tongue in his throat."

Canto V

Then we walked a while upon the well-lit
meadow, companionable as golfers
dawdling towards the nineteenth hole. The smell of
fresh-cut grass beguiled me, and the
even light was soothing to my eyes.
Their conversation was no more profound
than that of old friends enjoying an afternoon.
Including me in it, they did me honor.
Finally, Dante waved and said "*ciao*" and our trio
parted, Joyce to find his hidden

waters, we to the stenches and clamors below.
First we passed through a zone of silence.
I was occupied with thoughts, and he, with
what replaces thought for those who've
gone beyond it. Then, a distant gabbling,
like the geese that prematurely
whiten fields each autumn by Dead Creek near
Lake Champlain in tens of thousands,
a surf of voices, strengthened minute by minute
by imperceptible degrees

as we drew slowly closer to it, until
it wholly commanded both hearing and vision.
A stony field stretched wide. To the right, a corral.
In it a hideous anthropo-bovine
beast with a tail. Towards this, a few of the fallen
gathered, approached, too close: lashing,
that tail's coils whipped around one, dangled him near the
tufted ear. He screamed some sort of
confession. It flung him out of sight. "That's Minos,
tossing the traditionalists

where they belong in a manner they approve of.
Nowadays, the majority find their spots
in hell by more modern means." A row of desks
horizon to horizon striped
the slope below us. Behind each one, a chair; and
on the chair, a formless darkness,
featureless, uneasy as smoke, whose sluggishly
moiling margins shimmered dimly
as black velvet, crumpled, dimly shimmers.
Only they and nothing else

came close to gleaming in that place. We strolled
the line, and here and there at random
we paused to watch a process repeated ceaselessly
everywhere along it. A square of
friable dirt at each station spontaneously
mounded, puckered, farted forth a
human figure. "Here's the *anus mundi*,

the place the tunnel you saw ejects them."
So my guide. And each one, catching sight of
what roiled just across the table,

landed startled, graceless, stumbling, twisting
ankles, raising protective forearms,
staring straight ahead in horror.
This one grabs the table's edge
with stiffened arms, with lowered head and voice
dribbles his sorry stream of story;
while that one flings her elbows wide with shrill
defiance; another earnestly
explains, or sobs for pity, howls his anger,
spews her spite – all fixing their gaze on

or shifting it away from (but always back to)
or grimly altogether avoiding
the blank that receives their words. Then on each desk
a stack of paper forms appears.
The pages fill with what they've said as if,
approaching the horror in the chair,
the words fell dead and dropped. A smell of sweat
like stale socks fills the air. And now
the final plea, demand, request or curse
is uttered. All around the babble

presses in. Leaf by leaf, with a sibilant
rustle, the pages rise and fold and
coalesce, huge and vulturine, and

clasp their talons around the neck and
flapping lazy wings they carry the drained
and unresisting figure away.
Oh, the efficient long lines of them!
Trailing to so many points on the horizon,
dividing half the sullen sky. We followed,
barely able to pick our way through the

deepening dusk, uncertain always of seeing
what our eyes were looking at.
At last, ahead in a band of almost blackness,
I thought I saw red lights like coals
scattered from an upset barbecue.
Then they seemed to gutter, and a
sound of gusty winds – but no: they twinkled,
as if birds or was that moths,
huge moths fluttered at them. The lights were moving.
Rags of breeze brought the odor of

unwashed crotches. Then I saw what they were:
a horde of naked men and women
whose genitals glowed so you might read by them.
They shuffled uneasily around
each other, avoiding contact. Despite the blazing
wands and clefts and globes they carried,
their bodies – that is, their limbs and torsos and heads –
were strangely unilluminated,
merging chameleon-like with the rubbish and rocks
of their crepuscular habitat.

Sometimes they tried to shield or ease themselves with
fingers spread like wings, that jerked
away at each touch, singed. They gasped.
Heat approached me from the rear.
I whirled on a bearded face I'd never seen.
He muttered, "Yet I almost knew you
from behind. But what could bring you here,
not driven by a red hot poker?"
And then I knew him, and who these others were
who'd filled this circle, displacing Dante's

sweetly embittered lust-ridden lovers, a neighborhood
going downhill. It was his voice that
took me back to 1965.
A public shower-house at a State Park
beach, its concrete floor, its greyish dimness,
hissing heads, and fingers too softly to
startle kneading my thirteen-year-old shoulder,
and he whispered, that same voice as
smooth and lukewarm as the water sheeting us,
"Would you like me to soap your back?"

I escaped outside to a sun so brilliant
it sterilized the rocks. "You,"
I said, and stopped, and looked to Dante, who nodded
"go on." "You —" but words now failed me.
"I have no words for what you are." Sunless,
here, lit only by what ached,

flickering behind those helpless, shameful hands, an
unconcealable conflagration.
I hoped he'd unleash some revealing eloquence
like that of Dante's doomed Francesca,

a previous tenant. But I got this, instead:
after his father disappeared,
his mother's brother came to live with them.
One night the brother came home drunk.
In the morning, the sticky stuff drying on his
face was his blood; between his buttocks,
only partly that. The brother used him
for invasive pleasures until with the
passing years his pituitary accomplished
what his whimpering had not, and he

grew too big to need to submit. His mother
was no help. He told her. She said
that was her brother he was talking about.
He left home about the age I was
spooning with Vicky; passed a few decades with alcohol,
drugs, and all manner of numbness; had few
friends. He never hit the boys he found,
desiring above all else their carnal
initiation to be tender as his had
not been. When he was done, I vomited.

Canto VI

My senses vacant, abandoned outposts, I walked.
Until just now, he had been faceless.
The darkness had given me his face. Another,
more familiar, bobbed beside it
in my mind, like twin full moons whose pull had
warped the tides of my life. So I missed
a second chance to report what Dante had not.
Overpowered by grief for those whom
he'd found stricken here in love's name, he'd fainted,
and then he awoke in the circle below

with no idea how he had arrived there.
I walked through and simply missed it:
rocks and refuse, refuse and rocks
were all my complaining feet called me back to.
Then I heard a hissing, like freezing rain, and
above it a whining and growling, within it
continuous slithering, broken by loud engines
revving and idling. My eyes joined my ears and
saw that although the slope had trended downwards
now it swooped up. On top

triple-throated, raging, drooling Cerberus,
snatching figures out of the air from the
paper talons that carried them to him. Then he'd
toss them – first he'd worry them, and
then he'd fling them down into the pit whose
lip he pawed. We stood quite near him
in the frigid drizzle pissing down –
not too near – and gawked at horror.
I had to touch my chin to either shoulder,
peering sideways, to see where lack of

light obscured the ends of the grotesque pile.
Oh! they moved! The tangled limbs and
torsos slid and twitched, crawled and clung, as the
topmost burrowed for warmth against those
struggling upwards out of the stifling mass.
Those who'd landed farther away
were shoved by bulldozers towards the embankment we stood on,
compacting the mound and keeping it neat.
I thought of Henry Moore and photos of Auschwitz.
So we use art to distance ourselves.

In our times "bodies stacked like cordwood"
became a cliché, but shock is timeless.
I don't know how long it was before a face
emerged and greeted my guide in Italian,
"*Paisan'!*" and asked him, "What brings you back here?
A second visit! Such abundance!
Thank you for remembering me above! And

who is that with you, taking the air
that you, I see, have learned to do without?"
"I serve for him the office that the

ancient Roman served for me, Ciacco,
guiding him to where he's called by
those who used their mouths for something other
than to dig their graves. He knows your
fame; his homeland is named for our countryman
Amerigo Vespucci." "Oh, shit!
Another Yank. The place is lousy with them.
They've almost taken over. Sure, those
bare soles waggling over there
belong to a Philipino lady, who

left behind five hundred pairs of shoes,
but that cluster-fuck she's stuck in
owned the better part of Newport. For every
Kuwaiti playboy, the big dog throws in
a dozen McMansion cowboys from Texas alone.
But not even W can make that last."
He turned to me. "Would you like to know what happens
when the oil runs out and the greenback
falls to the Euro and the Chinese find something
better to do than fund your debt?

When W – " "No," I said: "A lot of good your
predictions did my friend here, when he was
shivering to death in Ravenna. Where I come from,

a country wasted with fat that willingly
welcomes its rule by greedy imbeciles,
industries exist to tell us
what will happen next and what to think
when what they said will happen next
does not. The people sit in their own filth,
transfixed by mirages. Tell me instead –"

But just then, Ciacco, the glutton and prophet, went limp,
sucked back into the heap the same way
someone slurps spaghetti. Beside me, Dante
bore the look of a person reminded of
painful things. It disappeared when he caught me
glancing at him. He said, "I was thinking of
Florence. What were you about to ask him?"
"How can eternal places change so?"
"The problem's your distorted vision. To you,
eternity looks the same as death

and both seem stagnant pools that time flowed into
before some avalanche cut them off.
Your science teaches otherwise: time ends in the
heat death of the universe,
but that is only one of many fates,
and all possibilities come to pass.
Eternity, therefore, is like an ocean with currents
that swarm and braid and branch and carry
many riders. Like you, each is bound for where he's
going and thinks there's nowhere else.

Or see it this way: when you were a child,
and maybe many times since then,
it delighted you to stand beside an
unruffled pond and pick out pebbles, the
flatter the better. One by one you'd fling them
skillfully, sidearm, snapping your wrist and
proudly counting the hops. That flat little pebble's the
world of your daily awareness. The pond is
everything else. You fly, you skim, you leap,
you skim that chilly otherness,

you leap a little shorter, skim again.
Every contact slows you and
propels undeviating flight to the next,
a little closer than the last.
Here the sandy pond bed glimmers; next, long
fingers of weed reach up at you;
next, a fish that mistakes you for a frog
rises to you with prickly teeth;
the water's warmer here, then colder; you jump
a little shorter. You sink. Each skip's

forever's moment rippled by your touch.
Mr. Belly knows nothing of that.
But how to pass here without being swallowed, I wonder?"
"We could walk. They're packed so tightly."
"Oh, no," he said. "You still don't understand.
You think the freezing rain, the airless crush

have causes external to these wretches: climate,
bulldozers. No. The law of this place is
they are their pain and they covet the comfort of flesh.
They'd use you to wrap their appetites in.

So we must find another way." And now he
gave me a taste of eternity,
deliberating long and silently.
Then, suddenly, he dived down smack
upon the landfill – a belly-flop! I sat
on his back, and he body-surfed across
the writhing mass. We regained our feet near an
idling 'dozer. A formless menace
filled its cab. Its radio seeped the music
that glazes shopping malls at Christmas.

Canto VII

Dante climbed to the cab, reached in and switched the
radio off, then cut the engine and
jumped. Although the ground was bumpy as
an egg crate, he soundlessly landed beside me.
The idling monster coughed to a stop, the blank in its
driver's seat immobile. Stillness
expanded around us like a bubble, as if a
clearing had opened in the forest,
as if a city block had just disappeared,
and we stood at the center, we

stood at the center of the wound, the hollow,
the place's empty unbeating heart
we could not leave no matter how far behind
we left the rumbling machines
the hissing rain, the groaning gasping mass.
Overhead the big birds flapped.
We followed, always downward. Sometimes, my feet
fell on unexpected dips and
flapped, too, but mostly I'd got the hang of
walking here. In Dante's silence

my mind wandered: home, subzero mornings,
lake unfrozen, mist so thick a
poor soul in the middle couldn't tell the
water from the air, the light's
diffusion through the blanketing vaporous clog
two score of minutes old, and looking
west – night's massy backside, unreadable unwritten
slate, sheets from heaven to earth.
Then faintly notes of lavender strike, and an almost
salmon orange pink that spreads

across and through the whitish gauzy veils
like swelling song. Here, the subtleties
all were grey and dun and dim. I kicked
the tarry thing before I saw it.
Smelled it first, too, a burst of vibrant reeks,
petrochemicals and more meaty
rot. Its feathers, snarled around a gash,
a beak, a vacant eye. Away it tumbled.
From behind me, crouching, loped
a skinny biped, yes, a human

chasing it. Quickly, others converged and fought for
possession. "Watch your step," my guide
reminded me as we edged away. "Get smeared
enough, and they'll come after you."
"But who are these – I want to call them people –
and what is that they're squabbling over?"
Widely scattered clots of them near and far.

"The predatorily avaricious.
So many of them spoke something like English. Now they
wander, ruggedly individual.

The place is littered with animal carcasses – road kill,
net-strangled dolphins, oil-soaked birds like that
gull you booted. They gather to feed on these."
We walked a ways without speaking.
Then I said: "Back there at the dead poets society,
you said I freed them by not believing.
But you believe, I know, that hell was harrowed
once, by Christ, and never again a
harvest until the Judgment Day. Don't you —
what do you mean, saying such things?"

From my irascible mentor, a kindly smile.
"Your anguish, son, becomes you. Such a
gap between the things you see and the things you
think were said, and in that gap
you get so pinched, so squeezed, trying to
find reality. Stay with the pain.
Every day is Judgment Day." He paused.
"This will solace you, perhaps.
They all are there – Homer, Aristotle,
Plato, Socrates, and Virgil,

Ovid, all the ones you named are there,
in that place of those whose virtues
filled their lives without including hope of

heaven. Disbelief obscures
from you what lack of hope condemns you to;
blinded by faith, I could not rejoice in
their rapturous, headlong flight through freedom's vacancies.
So they remain, captivated by
what they see by, and also escaped from the glare."
He chuckled. "As for you, my little

Twentieth Century secular Jewish Buddhist
son of man, well, your relation to
Christ's a mystery far beyond this long,
long dead, medieval Florentine poet."
This softly spoken last I barely heard.
My shoe struck something, sinking
slightly into it, and raised in my throat an
acrid ghost. I turned and heaved, and
when the spasms ended, wiped my lips
and looked for something to clean my hand on,

feeling hollow and shaky and heavy hearted,
like a tower made of straw
in which tolls a great, cracked bell.
I saw that he had led me onto
a flat and sodden plain, all pocked with pools
of something no one would want to wash in,
though faces broke the surface from time to time,
and hands, with violent gestures, and fists.
We squelched our way along the rims between
these pools, that grew to ponds; our path, more

deeply muddy, slippery, threaded a brownish
lacework ever more delicate;
at last, as best I could make out through the dark,
we'd reached a brink of unbroken filth,
its surface perturbed by slowly boiling faces.
"Here are those whom Virgil described
with words that so closely agreed with what I saw
I overlooked just how those seemingly
drowning were also swimming. Here, the sullen, the
angry, flail and bite in the muck, as

I reported. Sunken here are all whose
hatred of their world was mastered
only by their fear of leaving it.
Fear of breath's sweet cycle ceasing
made their lungs feel never full. They cursed
whatever could be lost, for passing.
The sun's clean photons, singing, bathed them and flew by,
cursed. But now their chests are swollen
full, and they may keep whatever they
can hold as long as they can hold it."

Canto VIII

"I remember a patio under a palm and a
lemon tree, a metal table
painted white I sat at afternoons,
reading the paper until I slept.
And I remember you. You used to hide
beneath the table from your *bobe*
when she tried to feed you a poached egg."
So crusted with half-dried muck he was,
I'd taken him for a log that had drifted ashore,
still half-submersed. But that burl was a nose, and

I knew this loose, deep rumbling voice that asked,
"Tell me, what is the meaning of this —
your feet are making slippers for themselves?"
I looked down. My ankles emerged
pale stalks from lips of mud as if rooted there.
It sucked and gasped as I raised my knees
to walk to him. I said, "I know you, too,
old man, old root stock, and it seems
to me you lived here long before you died there.
But where is Bubbie? Is she with you?"

"She may be somewhere, but she is not here.
Where should she be? How would I know ?
So maybe you'll visit longer than you used to."
"I'm sorry to say, not for long.
My feet are sinking because my heart beats, and this
shore can't bear that kind of weight.
I'm passing through to firmer and higher ground."
"You've got to go a long way down,
the way you're going, before you're going up.
Remember me, when you get there.

And who's this shade?" I told him about my guide.
"Pleased to meet you, Mister What-a-
Friend-We-Have-in-Jesus. A lot of *goyim*
drop in here to stay these days."
"And yet," riposted Dante, "Among us *goyim*
there are those who'd seat a Jew
beside us at that feast where one dish serves all."
"That's nice, Mister Pie-in-the-Sky."
"So death was your divorce?" I interjected.
"We wouldn't have known how to live apart.

You don't know how it was, the strength we gave
each other, even if it was only
the strength of mutual disappointment. Who else
could we rely on? In your country
you get off the boat and learn that it's like anywhere.
The only thing that working people
get from the bosses is what they can make them give them.

She destroyed her knees by kneeling,
scrubbing floors. The grout must be white as pearls.
That was the work that she could get.

She loved to dance. She couldn't dance. And I
was never home enough. I gave
myself to the union. Then they spit me out.
Why? You ask. One day I came to a
meeting ; thugs at the door wouldn't let me in.
These thugs belonged to the Party's bosses.
Also the union's bosses belonged to them, and
they belonged to Stalin. I
was loyal to those who disagreed with Stalin.
After that, I couldn't work in a

cloak shop, my trade, because I wasn't union."
Here Dante nodded sympathetically.
"So I went to work in non-union shops,
on dresses. I wasn't very skilled.
Forty hours for twelve to fifteen dollars.
Your *bobe* also worked non-union,
earned a little more. We fed our sons.
We came home every day to our
apartment building, where the neighbors called me
scab and *traitor*. Mothers leaned out their

windows and yelled at their children '*Why do you play with
the children of the renegade?*'
We heard our older son, your uncle, crying,

*Why do you hit me? Why do you punish
me for my father's sins?* And then the orders
changed again, they took me back,
the renegade, a paid official! For a
six month trial. Thirty-seven
years it lasted, and never did I rise
so high it made up for her knees."

Dante's voice sounded soft and light next to this.
"That city I loved above all others
was riven by faction. I was born to the Whites,
and married a daughter of the Blacks,
and attaining high office I banished the leaders of both.
But as you had no friend in the comrade
chief of the Workers' Paradise, the man who
held St. Peter's keys was Black in
his affections, so they exiled me,
to burn if I returned to Firenze."

The sound the old man made when thinking, a tuneless
basso hum, was his only response.
"Perhaps we should be moving on," I said.
And Dante: "Seven hundred years
ago, the Wrathful Boatman ferried us;
but though I've watched for Phlegyas, I see no
sign of his approach. The signal lights that
summoned him, the tower that held them,
are gone. Now I must consider our options."
He folded his arms and assumed the stolid

immobility of a surveyor's post.
The lightless expanse, its semi-solid
shoreline merging into seemingly limitless
filth, was silent. In my fancy,
the old man's drone – *HMM hmm HMM hmm* –
resembled a distant motorboat's engine
revving and laboring in choppy waters.
The sound of appraisal. The sound of danger.
The sound of a cat in its lair. The sound of my
uneasy breathing. Then: "A boat?

A ferry boat? You want to wait for him,
it's a long time you'll be waiting.
He sank out there when I was just a greenhorn.
You want to get across, I'll take you."
Astonished, I turned to the old crocodile.
"How ?" asked Dante, calmly, his tone
like one who has been waiting for another
to work out a problem and already knows
the answer the other will give. "*Nu*, you can't guess?
You will sit on my back, *mein ainikle*,

he will stand behind you, and I will swim.
Don't worry, it only looks like it boils.
Old anger is cold." So that is what we did.
I straddled his back, which bowed like a saddle.
He settled slightly less than I'd expected,
buoyant in his element.

Dante stood erect as a mast on his buttocks,
hands on my shoulders, while my *zaide*
slowly breast-stroked out into the channel.
At first, the gelid waters soothed my

feet, still burning from the multiple abuses
our trek across this wasteland had caused them, but
then it seemed like icy bands had clenched my
ankles, and my knees, and my
scrotum that was tightened even before I
lowered it in, and everything ached
below my waist, while submerged clumps of
something softly brushed my legs, and the
surface emitted an excremental stink.
By the time we'd crossed halfway, I'd

fallen half into a swoon, and failed to
see the hand reach up beside us
until it had curled around Dante's shin, and pulled, and
almost toppled him. A face,
distorted with rage, rose near us, howling hate.
My guide glancing down, then up to the clouds, said,
"Filippo Argenti, you won't have me this time,
either," and struggled to keep his balance.
Then a piece of cloud detached, and fell, like a
man-sized blob of steel wool formed of

shadows, covered the assailant's features and
scrubbed as if to erase them. His fingers

straightened and stiffened, and he sank, and so did
I, back to my semi-conscious
slump, where vaguely I heard my two companions
discussing politics. In the end,
it seemed more often than not that they agreed.
We finally reached a rocky shore.
Dante grabbed me under my arms and hauled me
up onto the shingle, while the man

to whom we owed this passage lay at the waterline
like a basking saurian. He cleared his
throat, and was about to speak when, like a
peregrine swooping on a fish, a
giant paper bird stooped and splashed and
bore him away into the murk.
I cried then. And Dante surprised me by expressing
compassion for one who cried for one of the
damned. And then, heart emptied, I tried to stand and
found my frozen legs were useless.

Canto IX

I'd been in car accidents, and sliced my thumb
to the bone with a knife, but never before
had I felt so certain that I was going to die.
Always there had been that path for
fear that hope bulldozes through the rubble.
But now the fear and I were trapped
together on this side of the wall between me
and whatever happens after
what comes next. I watched it dance. It grabbed me,
twirled me, but could lead me nowhere.

I thought, "Well, I can't follow." It made me laugh,
and the shivering stopped. Dante asked me
why did I laugh, and I said, "Don't you know?"
And he said, "Yes, but you should say it."
I said, "I'm dead. My legs won't move." And then I
noticed that already he had
paled. It yanked my attention outside me.
The stones I sat slump-shouldered on were
flattish, rounded, mostly palm-sized slate
of vari-hued grey, perfect for skipping

over the water, if one had been in the mood.
I thought of Dante's disquisition
on eternity: *I'm sitting on a
bed of moments here.* They pressed
smooth circles into the region where my torso's
chilliness met the nether numbness.
A few premonitory shivers rippled.
I staved off quaking by straining around
to look behind me. There I saw what the murky
air had conspired with my stupor to hide

while we crossed to this shore. My memory shows me
framed as in a picture, lying
at the bottom, separated by a
band of gray from the red that slashes
across the top; but through my eyes back then, the
stony strand bellied upwards a
quarter mile to a glow that ran side to side,
rubeous as inflamed gums,
fading only where vision faded." The wall of the
City of Dis," said Dante. "Hot iron."

"Can you bring me to it?" I asked. "I'm ready
whenever you are," he said, and sounded so
fondly amused that I untwisted back the
other way to look at him.
A shock! He stood quite naked, skinny and bony,
his elbows jutting as he tightly
furled his robe into a rope-like sling.

He passed it under my arms, and hauled me
effortlessly up the beach. But it was
a slow and painful trip for me.

Although I could not feel my feet, I knew from
jarring at my hips each time they
bumped the rocks. And radiating from his
shoulder to my cheek, no warmth.
At last he laid me down. I swooned a while.
Inside of me was a comfortable nothing.
I don't know how long I enveloped it.
I came back to the urgent fringe,
the rasping kisses of the tide of heat
the incandescent iron poured,

the subtle, insistent announcement of overwhelming
force. When first he laid me down, it
blanketed the side that holds my heart.
But now its malice stroked my back.
And as I lay there, dozing, dazed, his hands
rotated me gently as they could,
brought me full circle, face down again, and
my nerves told me, pins and needles, the
heat had licked and stroked me all around,
the way a whip does. And while he tended,

turning me like meat upon a spit
(a festal roast for the Fourth, Thanksgiving)
he crooned like a lullaby the song of Udrak,

"Master meditator, you who
fixed your mind upon the pearl indenting
your pure brow, and breathed its coolness,
changeless, unwound all the ragged flags of
thought to blow in nothing's breezes,
watched the lion's mane stir slow as
blades of grass, and all the while your

shaven head became unshaved, the stubble
grey, a million grey births boiling
from your scalp, and elongating greyly
dawn and noon and dusk and night.
Dawn and noon and dusk and night they grew,
a million grey births aging, while you
sat somewhere behind your eyeballs, taking
it all in and breathing out, and
breathing in and out. The mice had long since
learned to dance across your thighs, your

imperturbed and folded limbs their runways,
when their cousin rats moved in and
added yet another set of accents
to the polyrhythmic scurry.
Bolder, they would climb your form, their claws find
purchase on you, trigger nerves each
dawn and noon and dusk and night. Dawn and
noon and dusk and night they grow, a
million grey births aging, while you note
unmoved each prickling passing. Motes of

dust show where the air moves. Voices great and
small; all sorts of birds and bugs; the
sunlight's slide across the floor; the hiss and
creak, inaudible, of leaves and
stems that follow it; rain's varied kisses,
also wind's; the pulse of day, and
night's expanse – all weave the web in which
abides your calm awareness, wakeful,
resting as if in a hammock, dawn and
noon and dusk and night. Dawn and

noon and dusk and night it grows, a million
grey births aging. Then, at last
acceding to an itch, you know it's time to
stop, to start again. You rise like
steam, and walking past a window see
reflected havoc that the rats gnawed in
your hair. Your anger soars. But later,
standing over several still-warm,
long-tailed corpses, you recall that wide-eyed
vision ghosting on the glass, and

there's an inkling, so uneasy: one may
have his feelings without being had by
them, each dawn and noon and dusk and night.
Dawn and noon and dusk and night they
stir, a million grey waves, cresting, falling."
His reedy murmur faded. With it

my awareness waxed. It focused on my
legs. The heat of that horrid wall had
loaned them animation. I could move them.
Now began a long, dull march.

We kept the wall to our left, and stayed on the edge of the
cherry tinge it gave to the haze,
heading for a gate that Dante remembered.
Trudging for several quiet hours,
here and there we stopped while I replenished
myself; for there is food in hell,
as any dumpster diver knows. At last
we found a passway through the rampart,
twice my height and wide as sin and barred by a
gang of swirling burly nullities.

We faced them without speaking. His first time through here,
such a horde blocked Dante and an
angel saved him. I, however, am doubtful
of angels. "Ora pro nobis," I told him,
then feared I might have offended; but no, in Dante's
heaven he sat beside the Virgin;
so he stepped forward, declaiming, "Children of the
Father of Lies, I bring you one who
knows you well, a voter in Dubya's homeland,
where neither *That art Thou* nor *I*

Am What I Am nor *Do Unto Others* is
a stronger faith than *I Got Mine*:

America, where coffins come home unwelcomed,
where nonexistent weapons kill thousands,
where the President calls himself a tough guy
and flees from clouds, where terror has utterly
triumphed, and the only thing to fear is
fear itself, oh, omnipresent."
The gang's voice swelled like winds in the eaves, and I
drew near to my guide. "What are they saying?"

And he: "They conjure all the dreads that guide
your people: of germs, of anger, of youths of a
different race approaching, of vaporizing
that drops from the sky, of brilliance, of the
void at the center, of pain, of the panic of being
unsexed, uncertain, unemployed, and
seeing yourselves as you fear others see you –
naked, fat, unloved, unloving ;
of One you know will take it all away."
"Oh land of the free and home of the brave!

The Prince of Frauds squats at the desk of him
who said *the buck stops here,*" I cried.
"Yes, our beloved!" moaned the mob, "who said,
when cold black waters came to town,
but nobody thought the levees would break! Such laughter
as we laughed that day in Hell,
only the Big Easy's floating bodies could hear."
"But we both know that lies have only
the power their servants give them," my guide responded.

"Come!" he called to the shifting ranks that

barred our way. "Now let us pass. For we
will need no angel to clear you, if this
is willed where what is willed must be!" And while I
pondered what he could mean by that "if,"
he paused, like one who awaits a reply, then turned and
saw me wavering, hesitating, and
opened his mouth, but thinking better of it he
grabbed my elbow, whirling faster, and
flung me headlong forward, stumbling speechless and
flapping my arms among the blanks.

Canto X

It had been like walking through cobwebs, if cobwebs
reached right through the walker and mocked him.
My hearing cleared before my sight returned.
At last I saw Dante slapping his thighs.
"You looked like a man assailed by bees," he gasped,
slowly regaining his composure.
"How you struggle with falsehood! To laugh or to weep,
it's hard to choose. But, since you were winning,
I had to celebrate your triumph. Oh, my."
He wiped his eyes with the back of his hand.

The demons were gone, except for a few black strands
that stuck to my clothing. I plucked them off.
And from that harrowment I might have emerged
enough to smile with him, except for
our sobering setting. Between a slate sky
and basalt plain a brownish haze
like the one that hides Hollywood from the City of Angels
enveloped rectangular objects I learned
were large and distant only by walking toward them,
as the gnarly rock was devoid of

features that might have aided perspective.
Treading our way through this chafing terrain,
I wondered aloud at what they had said, of levees
broken and bodies floating. This was
August of 2005. He replied, "Recall what
I wrote Farinata told me.
Come quei c'ha mala luce, they see
down here the past and future only,
the present to them is a blooming buzzing blur
they never will grow to clearly perceive.

Some will scruple, squinting, to distinguish
what is coming from what has been.
Others, like your informants, do not care."
Pondering this, my thinking ran on
two diverging tracks, until at last
anxiety shunted me onto one.
Which then proliferated so that soon
I shuttled back and forth throughout
an entire mental switchyard. Farinata,
whom Dante'd found entombed and burning

here, had espoused the heretic belief that
at death life's sentence ends full stop.
To which I'd always said that I don't know
while inclined to agree with Farinata.
But being here proved – what? Anger's freezer
burn had doubtless crippled me,
but was that in this life or in some other

connected by threads as thin as cobwebs?
And so on, each thought fueled like the boiler
of a steam train by the flames that

had, in Dante's days, licked so many.
Then, startling me, a voice demanded,
"Do you know why you have been brought here?"
Booming, metallic, and quite near by.
I raised my eyes and found its source in a box-like
structure of rusty steel, taller by
half a head than my leader, open-topped.
A hand raised over the side commandingly
waved us closer. Dante gestured me quiet.
"Who is it who dares to ask?"

His voice was gentle; his tone was anything but.
"Lavrenti Beria." "And who is with you?"
"Kang Sheng, Torquemada, Hermann
Goering, Isabella who
expelled the Jews and Moors, Teymur Bakhtiar,
Augusto Pinochet and others."
"That should answer the question that you have been
withholding," Dante said to me.
"We heard you approaching. We listen for anyone coming,"
the voice continued. "We are surrounded

by fiends and uncertainty. Sometimes for amusement
they cause the sides of this bin to close;
they squeeze whatever is in us out. Silence

alone preserves us from their attention.
But you are unlike them – your steps have weight."
"Not mine. I escort one whom power
summoned while yet alive. I speak for him
because you forfeited ever hearing
living speech the day that you first sought to
produce it from screams." "Well is that so?

Then know, my breathing comrade, here's
a place reserved for Alberto Gonzales
and one for General Geoffrey Miller, too."
"How did you know ?" I blurted out.
"I can always smell a Yank!" he crowed.
"Too bad the god that you served failed,"
retorted Dante quickly. "Come on. Let's leave
this trash to their compactor. On them
all words are wasted." "Wait! Wait! *American*!"
pleaded a new voice from within,

"Didn't the Red call you American?"
"May I speak with this one?" I asked.
"His accent says that he's your countryman,"
my leader mused, "but keep it brief."
I said, "Your tools were subpoenas, not thumbscrews;
the honorable junior senator
from Wisconsin, do I have that right?"
"I had the pleasure of being called that.
Now I am pleased to be remembered. Thank you."
"Oh, you made your mark, alright,

like a dog on a carpet, and just as shamelessly.
You would be proud of the crew who've followed the
tracks you left, though they might hesitate to
acknowledge their debt to you in public.
Their President was a pilot the way you were a
tailgunner; his bogeys are foreign devils;
with manly mannerisms he musters terror.
What he really believes who knows?"
"Good luck to them when they discover the reins
they thought they gripped so firmly are

a tail, and the yellow eyes are turned on them.
Chased me right back down the bottle.
Did I believe there really were two hundred
commies in the State Department?
Hell, why not?" "Enough?" my leader asked.
"Just one more thing," I said, and slapped
a big black button on the end of the bin. "A token
of respect for all they accomplished."
A moment of silence. Then I knew my guess
was right. The clanking and grinding began.

"Enjoy your hollow victory while it lasts,"
Beria's voice, scornful, echoed.
"Sooner or later the sides withdraw, and we,
empty to begin with, emptied
of our emptiness, *reconstitute*, full of
all the pain that brought us here.

Nothing you might do could add to that."

"Maybe so," said Dante, "but now,

commingle thy substance, thou winnower of souls."

We left them alone to their ghastly exhalations.

Canto XI

Dante hurried down the broken slope.
I labored, but couldn't match his footwork.
If we were racing to the palely gleaming
marble box he led me towards,
he was the winner, but when I joined him there a
minute later, heavily panting, he
greeted me absently, as if unwilling to
be distracted from thoughts he carried.
Half a dozen paces away, he stood
alone, arms folded, ruminating.

Although, as I caught up, he rested his chin
on the edge of the box's slab side, I had
to stand on tip-toe to see within to the bottom.
"Look for yourself," he'd muttered. I'd balked: the
lid, a slice of stone about eight feet long,
half that in width, and six inches thick,
hovered a couple of feet above the rim,
unsupported, its rabbeted edges
clean and sharp. *But he didn't bring me here to
have my skull crushed in*, I thought.

Still I hung back. It reminded me of Magritte.
I clung to that association,
contemplating the monstrous, suspended weight as
if it were a painting, until my
curiosity took my trust in my teacher
by the hand and led me forward.
As soon as the greater dimness beneath the lid
touched my brow, I heard a voice
composed of many voices, all familiar,
jumbled and garbled. Words also tumbled

across an opened book that was carved on the chest
of the figure lying in the crypt.
Among the voices, my voice, and phrases of mine
fleeted through the writings like leaves in a
river in spring's spate, surfaced then drowned.
Gradually, the sounds and writings
merged into simple clarity, like a final
chord or peroration: "HE FEARED
TO BE EXPOSED." The letters' wriggling rose
to a writhing, exploded in scribbles, and vanished.

I saw that the fingers which held the pages they'd traced
belonged to an effigy of me.
The open eyes and placid face showed nothing.
So artfully was the granite carved,
some hairs of the moustache strayed across the lip
as if untrimmed; the coarse grain faintly
swelled in a line at the base of the neck where my scar is.

The left thumb's cuticle was split.
Half the right big toenail was thickened and darkened.
The penis was chipped. Cracks had formed.

One ran along the nose, but not quite parallel
to the bridge, and opened at the
mouth like a hare lip. A few black ants crawled from it.
Fascinated and appalled, as
helpless to move as a dead man's mirror image,
I gazed at it. Taking my arm, Dante said,
"Step back," and pointed at the lid, which quivered
like something seen through heat from afar.
Still I dallied, mesmerized. He dragged me
away, then, to where I was shocked awake

by a stench that streamed, as startling as smelling salts,
over the brink of a cliff. Retreating to
where it was barely bearable, we paused there.
We must descend, he explained, but first must be
deadened by olfactory fatigue.
"Meanwhile, listen: you who live,
impelled like sailboats by the winds in all
their charming variety, each of you drags
an anchor through these grounds. Sometimes, some catch.
That tomb is a window to the image

of what might moor the one who looks inside it.
Take heart. The kedge you saw is small,
and crumbles. With every step along this path,

you pound it into dust." "To drift?"
"Beyond the need for navigation." A swirling
cloud of particles of thought blocked
access to my tongue. Then I recalled his
gruff withdrawal as I'd approached.
It stung enough to cut a way for words.
"You might have told me this before

I saw myself laid out with weeds growing through me.
What did you see that made you forget you're
here as my guide?" "I saw nothing,
of course. What else would you expect?
But memory ballasts even the freest sailors,
and I looked in here once before.
The ground tackle takes its form from the habits of mind
of the man or woman to whom it's tethered.
In there I saw Pope Anastasius burning.
Of him, I'd read that bishop Photinus

convinced him that my Savior was created
by a penis spurting in Mary.
I will tell you no such thing is possible.
I have known the virgin mother.
But to the point: in my youth, when Beatrice,
who opened for me the meaning of love,
had died, I sought philosophy's consolations
and followed Photinian reckonings,
believing the highest good might be sought and found
in sweet, moist depths. So I was fouled."

"Are you trying to tell me that sex is evil?"
He gave me the look a teacher gives
a very slow student. "No; but he
who thinks with his crotch is apt to come
to wrong conclusions." I know someone who, had he
been there, might have said, "Thank you, Mister
Fortune Cookie." But it struck me that, in
hell, an aphorism encapsulates
pain, andso I swallowed the impulse to speak, and
renewed affection filled my eyes.

"Now," he said, turning towards the parapet of
jagged boulders that rimmed the brink,
"I think you are fortified against their smell
where we must go." But hell makes a snare
of everything ; I wanted to linger in this
air of freshened understanding.
"Wait," I said, casting for something to hold him. He smiled,
and my conviction that he knew
exactly what was on my mind confused me
all the more: what could I say?

"As a fellow poet, and, well, student of
yours, I apprehend the distinction you
draw between creation and reproductive
biology, but…" "My son, you'd find this
all much easier if you'd stop insisting that
at each point, on some level,

there must be a sense in which we agree.
Such thinking leads to the trash in those bins.
Immaculate conception's no metaphor,
to me; for you, it's nothing else.

Remember what your Godel and your Whitman
teach of contradiction. Embrace it."
"No," I said, "No. That's not it, at all.
Well, not exactly..." He smiled, and I knew
that what I could not reach in him was just
the thing that I must learn to love.
And vice versa. "She was so sweet,"
he said, "I howled with it. I followed words
to her, and language died. And now I've repaid
your desire with interest, we should go."

Canto XII

Chunks of granite and quartzite clogged the ravine that
slashed the escarpment to its base
six hundred feet below us, steeper than
the Long Trail's drop to Route 9 near Bennington.
"It looks all freshly fallen," I said, and he:
"Two thousand years ago, this crag
was rent, so Virgil told me, when my Lord
passed through here, gathering souls. Before,
these rocks remained intact." "How ironic,"
I pointed out, "that your Lord's passing

has opened new ways for men to descend into malice."
"Save your breath," he said, "You'll need it."
Then down he flitted, skipping from perch to perch,
like a child who terrifies his parents
by traipsing through hazards, oblivious, as if
mortality never will make its grab.
I watched until he reached the bottom and beckoned.
He cupped his hands to his mouth and hollered,
"Go the way I went!" *Yeah, right,* I thought.
I contemplated touching my toe to

this column of rocks, forty stories tall,
arrested in mid-cascade for one
extended moment, untrodden, unweathered, unsettled,
randomly frozen and mousetrap ready
for living weight to trigger its resumed plunge.
Extending a foot, I gingerly prodded
a flattish rock some inches below the brink.
It seemed firm enough and soon it
held me. The next one teetered the second my arch had
flattened to it. And so it went,

groping step by step, never sure of my
ground until it was beneath me, and
not always then. I balanced on the edge of a
slab and felt it shift, leaped back and
watched it slide away in a cloud of dust.
Nothing was bedrock, nothing safe.
The nerves from my toes to my brain, strung over quivering
knees and aching back, seemed long and
slow to signal as transatlantic cables.
Thought's braided cycles slowed and

concentered on one repeating desire, which I
rode like a chute: to keep my flesh,
to behold Victoria with eyes that could blink,
to meet her later rather than now.
It carried me down. At last, when my feet crushed pebbles
into the unmoving dirt, Dante's
welcome startled me, and I was slow to

recognize him. "Teacher!" I whispered.
He stood by a huge mound of black-haired hide; bones protruded
from it. "The Minotaur,"

he said, and we walked silently for a while.
away from the cliffs, and towards a distant
roaring, whose source was hidden in the murk,
as was, very soon, the Minotaur.
My arduous descent had driven my spirit so far
within that for now it was content
to patrol no farther than the happily intact
borders of my skin, so I did not
ask how the monster became a broken bone bag.
When the source of the roaring was almost

within the limits of my vision, the next
vague objects preceded it there:
big round blobs with skinny straight outshoots.
Bloated, stiff-legged equine carcasses.
Where the neck should arch to the head, a box-like
rib-cage, a knobby skull – centaurs!
"Drowned," said Dante, "and cast upon this shore."
Horrible and stinking. And there, at last,
the surf rolled at us in perfect curls, black in the
low light with a red sheen, a

great sound like giant books ripping,
steaming and spuming and smelling of iron,
salt and corruption, flung on the beach and hissing

back to the rollers that flung it again.
"Two hundred and seventeen years before my brother
Martin Luther (I call him my brother
although I never lived to enter his Order)
nailed his heart to the Wittenberg door, I
stood here, on this spot, and saw a sluggish,
boiling river, easily forded.

In it stewed the violent, some to their ankles,
others over their heads, according
to the grief they'd caused. That stream began to
swell around the time Martin wrote.
I often chide him now, should he have written
poetry more than polemics, the number of
wars fought in his name might equal the number of
wars fought in mine." "America's native
holocaust dates to those days, too," I offered.
"Yes, and the Middle Passage filled the

river to its banks like a hurricane. It
overflowed with your Civil War, for
whose dead Lincoln weeps in Purgatory, a
lamed vovnik, a boddhisattva.
Twenty centuries after one was born who
could have taught you better, it rose
faster than the Bay of Fundy's tides,
sweeping over those poor creatures
you saw reeking on the strand. They'd ventured,
when the murders briefly receded,

to the mudflats that your Gilded Age laid
bare. There Sarajevo caught them.
Who remembers vengeful Nessus, worthless
Pholus, mighty Chiron? Few.
Still this tide, unebbing, shoves their corpses
towards the cliffs – and then: *vernichtung*.
Maybe you will make all hell an ocean.
Our task now is to get across."
A paper bird passed overhead and dropped its
load a hundred yards offshore.

We could faintly hear the yell, but not the
splash. I realized that three or
four of them had flapped by while we talked.
Dante stuck two fingers in his
mouth and shrilled, a bosun's whistle. Banking
sharply, the creature veered to us and
dipped its long, thin beak, then raced away. Its
legs trailed like a crane or heron.
"Now we wait," he said. How good it was
to drop the burden, to do nothing.

Waiting released us into intimacies so
sweet and unexpected, that now I
smile at remembering how I smiled, although I
remember so little of what we said,
leaning together on that livid margin,
nostrils clogged with its heavy tang,

dancing away from the surf's blistering lick.
I sweated in the swelter. At times
it might have been a summer's walk on the beach,
though dark, and red, and smelling of death.

He was about to tell me which of his own lines
was his favorite – I had told him
Allen Ginsburg's was "boxcars boxcars boxcars" – when
something approached us through that gap between
optical data and the mind's possessing of it,
that same abyss from which white clouds of
sails and massive hulls appeared outside
Pacific reefs to islanders who
could reach for nothing in their world to connect
to what was there, so said they could not

see the vessels, laden with cannons and pox for
paradise. Our visitation,
unlike theirs, was wholly benign, so equally
out of place. The brumous air
disclosed him like a poorly executed
special effect, in definition,
tone and texture distinct from all around him.
His tight-pored skin, his coarsely woven
linen loincloth, sparsely stubbled skinny
chest, his long, broad nose that

angled over his moustache, his forehead sweeping
up and up, his eyes behind their

circular glasses so sad and bright. "Mahatma," my
master said, and bridged the worlds.
"We are honored." "Oh, stop," replied the man.
"That is how you think he thinks that
I should be addressed. But I was called to
perform a function. Shall we begin?"
Briskly he turned to face the heaving sea and
tossed his walking stick at an onrushing

wave that might have scalded him head to toe. The
cane was still dry when it hit the ground,
rattling. An avenue had opened before us.
We followed him in. The swell and chop of the
surface soon were far overhead, but the walls
we walked between through heat like a sauna
shimmied and bulged. For distraction, I asked,
"Why does sexual violence land one
up there, lighting the dark, instead of here?"
Our saviour answered. "What does he seek,

this rapist of yours? He thinks he has found it, but look:
all he sees is his own ugliness
pinned beneath him. He sees no person there,
only his own repulsive shadow.
And think: what is the means he is driven to use
to violate and exert power
over this mirage? The force that connects, that
binds one body to another
beyond words, that fuses them in a third.

He seeks rebirth, to make himself whole.

This cannot be accomplished by harming others,
of whom, after all, we are a part.
Rape is *satyagraha* upside down.
So, you see, who cleaves to the mirror
differs from him who would smash it. 'Who takes a life
destroys a world.'" "I COULDN'T COME,
SO I SLIT THE FUCKING BITCH'S THROAT!"
a head extruded from the wall
gargled at us. "I am sorry to hear it,"
answered Mahatma, and hurried us past.

Canto XIII

It makes no sense to speak of time in hell's
continuous, trapped and desperate present, but
we had walked long enough to make it hours
later when Dante said, appalled,
"There once were shallows in this place where lesser
evils soaked their aching feet."
He cast a speculative glance at me, but held
his peace. "This path avoids such places,"
said our leader. "They are not the fords that
you remember. Our friend would find them

much too steep and dangerous. The coral would
lacerate him terribly. Falling
into this pond from the heights, those who end here
touch bottom, and there debris from
lives they shattered encrusts them. Hitler, Stalin,
Mao, Mussolini, Tojo,
Pol Pot, Generals Bonaparte, LeMay and Dyer, the
butchers of Wounded Knee and Armenia; so
many foundations for an ever-growing
archipelago. Bagosora's

atoll soon will join it, just awash and
miserably crowded with flightless flamingos."
Amid this cataract of names, the sense crept
over me of being followed.
Last in line, I peered back, but our channel's
wavy walls and muddy floor were
empty. Mahatma caught me looking, and said,
"Yes, we are trailed by one who has bound
himself to me much closer than a brother,
poor man. You will see him soon, when we

come to the place where he has no will to go."
Almost imperceptibly,
the path we trudged began to lead us upwards.
I'd lowered my eyes like a penitent,
and when I felt myself lean slightly forward,
breathing harder, I thought I was tired.
But suddenly my head entered the region
of clashing, fluid crests and troughs.
Like a historian, I watched their play, delighted,
forgetful the lovely, shifting patterns

were boiling blood. At last the dirt beneath
my feet had lifted my head above
the surface far enough to see a distant
figure leaping like a porpoise
in and out of the tumult we had passed through
and keeping to the right of our track
although the waves rejoined not far behind us.

I pointed it out to Gandhi. "Godse,"
he said, "who jumped into this river expecting
they'd scatter his ashes in another."

We rose from fetor to the fresh stinks of a
hardpan beach in clotted darkness.
Gandhi turned around, as if to wade back,
extending his arms palms up. Three times
above the ripping surf he flicked his fingers
and called to join him a man whose torso
suddenly rose from the foam where we had walked.
The man's face twisted. "You had to be stopped,"
he said, it seemed in sorrow. "Perhaps," said Gandhi,
"but what made you think a bullet would do it?"

"With reverence for your service, your service was over.
I was correct to ensure that," he said,
and dived back under the tide. "I fail again,"
said Gandhi, as if he'd expected no better.
"It's terror of leaving the bath that keeps them in there.
What can you do against that?" said Dante.
"A whole world drowning like Marat," I said.
"No, he is in the grove beyond
the dunes," wheezed an unfamiliar voice.
"Come over here. I'll tell you where."

I looked around. We'd landed by a shallow
cove, much like a mangrove swamp if
stripped of all its moss and leaves and seen on an

overcast, moonless night, the barren,
stunted trees arrayed with six-inch thorns.
I shifted my weight, but "Don't!" commanded
Dante. "These are suicide bombers, pickling their
roots. She'll drop a limb on you...
as if to say, you're so important, and
I do not know how else to touch you,"

he added, then commanded "Follow me," leading
over dunes as sharp as saw teeth.
Upon the last dune's blank brow sprouted a thicket
like thin hair, with one tree down
like a shock across the unruly forehead of someone
I thought I might find here, his skin the
negative image of this place, so white;
broad lips, broad cheekbones, eyes that were always
anxious to laugh, a loving heart, his words a
little awkward, his tongue a little

thick, who'd come to us from somewhere else.
Don't romanticize him. Something
of a clown, a tinge of doofus dogged him.
I was absent the day they dragged him
out of school, bumming on acid, flailing,
screaming, men all over him.
The teachers were horrified, the EMTs
professionally competent.
He left in the clutches of dread and thorazine.
After that, the movie screen he

found himself the wrong side of, forever, the
back-projected human world
no matter how he charmed and joked he could not
flatten into, and I marvel
at the strength with which he neatly arranged
so many things so many years:
high school graduation, college, Psy.D
(what else?), job, career, and girlfriend;
until he neatly arranged his watch and wallet
on the front seat of his car and

stepped in shiny shoes off of that bridge.
God bless you, Doron, I heard myself think.
Then I awoke to where we were. *In hell,
among his kindred spirits.* What?
I had begun to imagine myself an ignorant,
blundering, unconscious deity.
Limbo was vacated, lovers liberated,
predators cauterized off, the demons'
fangs collapsed into scribbles, all by the force of
my sovereign disbelief – but

here the victims continued to be damned
because their bodies had outlasted
their souls' endurance? At whose order? Not mine!
"Don't tell me they're punished for spurning
some cosmic fascist's unreturnable gifts.
If that's the case, then show me my cell.

Non serviam! If that's the quality of
your justice and love, my place is here!"
This last in a strangled yelp. "Oh, dear," said Gandhi.
"Punished, you say? What have they taught you?"

"Don't look at me," said Dante, "He is a most
frustrating student." He turned to me.
"Your sense of rightness is offended. Frightened,
you sputter silly expostulations,
elevating your discomfort into
an epic Star Wars struggle, erasing
all the world but you and your Dark Lord.
That error's as common as mulch in this grove.
So I reported divine wrath endlessly pouring ;
certainly that is what it looked like

back in the day, but since then you have taken a
larger measure of human abilities.
Consider your science. It prefers the elegant
explanation. Does observation
reveal to you a single thing in this
metropolis a billion souls
wrongly employed who labored millenia could not
have created for themselves?
You've slapped together your shantytown, and now
you want an Architect to blame?"

Into the following hush, a distant baying
entered, as of hounds. I raised my

gaze from where embarrassment had lowered it.
An apple orchard in late November,
I thought, the fruit long gone off leafless limbs.
The harpies Dante'd reported tearing
the foliage to increase pain were long flown, helpless
to break through Thanatos' analgesic.
Beneath each tree, a mound of clothes. They stank of
despair. "They chose to plant themselves here,"

I said, "I get it." The baying grew louder and closer.
A naked man came dashing through the
grove, breaking twigs and branches that
protested only by snapping. He dived
into a pile of men's wear, pinstripe suits and
boxer briefs. He burrowed as if to
hide among them. "Who are you?" I asked.
"I was a real estate developer,"
he panted. Then the animals fell on him and
something scorned exacted revenge.

Canto XIV

Gandhi paused at the edge of the dismal wood.
"I go no farther," said the old
hunger-striker. "Here I say goodbye."
Turning into the trees, he was gone.
Just so, I've seen a black bear amble across
the road and dive into the thicket
and suddenly become invisible.
Dante and I hesitated.
A featureless waste of rippling sands met the tree line,
where we stood, as a floor meets a wall.

Ash flakes drifted sparsely from the sky.
One streaked my palm with greasy soot.
A vigorous stream, bright red and thick as gravy,
spurted from the woods to our right in a
channel lined with blocks of stone as straight as the
Corps of Engineers could have made it.
"There lies our way," said Dante. "We'll walk on the riprap."
Elevated shoulder high,
this route saved me from slogging through miles of sand whose
grains my guide could have floated atop.

It was free of the showering cinders, that also
oddly left no trace on the desert
but smirched whoever walked there. We traveled in silence
until I asked, "What was that look
you gave me, back in the depths?" And he replied,
"I wondered at your bloody times.
You know I left the flesh some twenty years
before the Black Death flayed so many.
That scourge was visited upon its victims.
But in your day, you cursed yourselves."

"When I was small, in school, we kneeled in the hall,"
I answered, "our foreheads touching the cold,
metal lockers. We waited quietly.
I could hear the other children
breathing and the teachers' shoes squeaking
behind me in the hallway, a long time.
At last, the buzzer told us we could raise
our heads, go back to class, it really
was a drill. No bombs, today. They called it
civil defense, not child abuse.

So now the nation cowers the way it was taught to.
Fear is the heritage we share. The
puritans' god was a wrathful god, and in the
land of spacious skies and amber
waves of grain the anthem we sing before
they throw the first pitch is not *Take
Me Out to the Ball Game* but a celebration

of having endured bombs bursting in air.
Slaves and slaveholders, natives and immigrants bound by
ropes of fear, whose children fling missiles

into shelters full of fearful Baghdadis."
Sometimes a question releases something
that takes us beyond the words we give in answer
to places lit by other lights.
Thus preoccupied, I noticed but failed to
see the figures we approached
until we stood just over them. They huddled
in a ring below us, speaking
animatedly, and punctuating
their talk with abrupt and emphatic gestures.

They were so grimy they seemed to be clothed. Perhaps
that hid from me what was untoward.
"Who are these?" I asked. "Ssh! Listen and watch."
At Dante's words a bulky man
straightened his back and turned from the group, and my stomach
flipped when I saw what his shoulders carried
over to our feet. What do you see
when I say faceless? Maybe a smooth
ovoid, perhaps with a cute potato-ish bump where the
nose should be, and dimples for eyes, and a

lipless, toothless hole, of course, for a mouth.
Focus on that hole. Surround it with
bruised, swollen, pulped and ragged tissue.

Some of the blood is congealed, some runs.
It's said that Serbs would beat their Bosnian captives
beyond individual recognition
until they were brokenly, broadly, barely human.
Like this. Words frothed from him. The voice
was like a wind among rocks. He spoke at length,
and when at last my comprehension

stumbled into action, my horror eroded
to astonishment to hear
the two of us berated for our "errors"
by this pitiful wreck, who offered
"correction" and with each correction raised
a quivering arm and smashed his fist
into what uncorrected had been his face,
exclaiming "nono!" with each punch.
Once, I had to step back to escape the spatter.
Of what he said, I remember little.

The blows with which he destroyed his person also
drove from my mind the ideas that drove them.
"Who is this?" I repeated, and sidled behind my
guide for protection. "Pius the Ninth,"
Dante answered, "and in his circle, those who
presumed to rise above fallible mankind
and speak for god. Here's Jim Jones, a gaggle
of Southern Baptists, the ayatollah
who lowered the fatwah on Salman Rushdie, Hindu
fanatics, a gang from the Thirty Years War."

"Reverend Robertson and Mullah Omar shall
join our humble passion play,"
added the Pontiff. "Are you that same one who
enhanced Rome's quality of life
by building a ghetto to keep its Jews out of sight?
How nice to meet you here," I said.
"Oh, Alighieri, curb that whelp you drag
behind you, barking and molesting
honest people. But, since you have brought the
cur to this sandbox, let me whip him

just a bit. Atheist Yankee Hebrew,
soon you'll find how thin your wall is,
separating church and state." And Dante:
"As you learned how easily the
wrong that I ascribed to Constantine
could be undone. A shame you didn't
do it yourself, but left that work to others.
Now, my son, we must be moving.
To trade words with these is to make a bad bargain."
As we walked away, I asked,

"How did he know your name?" "Having authored
a popular guide through these parts, my services
have been called upon more than once. The last,
your colleague and countryman, Longfellow,
upbraided him quite nicely for his Confederate
sympathies and for snatching that child from its

Jewish parents because a maid had baptized it.
Did you think your trip is unique?"
He paused a moment, laughed, and so we strolled
companionably chatting. I told him,

"I'm thinking of someone I thought I might meet, down here,
in one of the places we've passed. He suffered
a stroke in middle age. It was like lightning
splitting an oak, when one half lives and the
other hangs from the living. Never mind
what he was before. His past was
cleaved from his present, as useless as an arm,
a leg, and one side of his face.
I knew him only after. When I was a child,
he'd bring me presents: a broken watch,

a pair of socks; and once he called me *Adonys*!
That was doting! When I was grown,
I visited him." How to describe to Dante
the urine-and-chemical scented halls,
the ranks of wheelchairs facing inwards from unwashed
windows, the televisions' cacophony?
"In the nursing home," said Dante, "That is
where you keep them. Please go on."
"They brought him to me. We sat outdoors at a little
metal table. He said nothing.

He never talked much, any more. They said
he liked to pinch the nurses' aides,

as if to say, there's life in the old goat yet.
But nobody knew where his mind had gone.
I kept on looking around. His eyes were still.
I told him he'd been my childhood hero.
Don't bullshit me, he said. I asked if he had
regrets. The answer came slowly. *My marriage.*
Then he wouldn't say any more, though I prodded.
I saw him again, a few years later:

his ninetieth birthday, alone in a chair in the corner.
A roomful of people, celebrating.
I kneeled beside him. He made a noise, a kind of
articulate grunt, and his good hand pulled –
well, clawed at the arm of his chair. I knew what he wanted.
Have you ever lifted driftwood,
and been surprised at its lightness? That's how I felt,
raising him and helping him stagger
one or maybe two steps forward before a
clutch of concerned relatives gently

wrested him from me and back to his chair, chiding.
Did I know how brittle his bones were?
What if he fell? I thought, At ninety years,
he's falling already. Let him enjoy it.
Two years later, he was dead. The doctors
wanted to take his cancerous prostate.
He insisted that part be untouched; they could clear his
eyes of their glaucoma clouds
instead. They put him under and took it all.

After that, he refused to eat."

"Your love should show you the answer. Your world is broken.
Your Jewish sages teach that its nature is
to be shattered; and how else could the faith
that I hold true reside in trinity?
To be whole is to be ready to leave
for good and all; you call it *tikkun*,
the healing of the shards. A wolf in a trap
may free himself by leaving a part.
Your grandpa left his body, sundered and fierce.
He's where you thought, but mostly elsewhere."

Canto XV

I rushed and stumbled atop the rough-hewn, irregular
granite blocks that paved our way
along the bubbling stream, hard pressed to keep up
with the rapid, even stride of
someone unconcerned about stepping in cracks and
twisting an ankle, scared to look up when
he would call my attention to another
miserable sodality, near or far,
battering away their unwanted humanity,
stubbing a toe whenever I did.

After a while I didn't bother to look,
eschewing these scenes of monotonous self
destruction for the sake of my poor feet,
whose progress upon the pavers I monitored
closely until my attention was led astray by that law
by which the mind deprived of distractions
creates its own. So I remembered a walkup
apartment I'd shared downtown above
a waterfall with a man who was misnamed "gay"
for his love of men, the frantic, drunken

nights he threw himself into arms mismatched
except for passion, the town outside
so cold to me who merely lived with him,
his room all purple draped and pillowed.
I remembered also a boy who swam
the lonely length of my thirteenth year.
Several dozen of us shivered beside the
pool, awaiting commands. Submerged in
blue were lines of dark green tile, and yellow
nylon ropes that ran above them

laid out lanes to channel our exertions. They
wavered slightly, the ropes and tiles, with
agitation from the previous class that
gently humped and hollowed the water.
Captive poolside with the rest, I studied
manliness as taught by men who
liked to order teen-age boys to compete. I
watched his brown and slender torso,
gleaming wet, the muscles smooth as milk, his
arms outstretched to pierce the surface,

forever after suspended in memory
as then he seemed in mid-air, as if
the upwelling smell of chlorine held him there.
Two years later, in bed, I rehearsed
delicious frictions a certain girl inspired me
to imagine, he intruded,
displacing a never actually sighted nipple.

        I thought, *I ain't no queer.* But then
I thought *how different imagining is from doing*
          and embraced this freely offered

    loveliness, sank with rising energy into it,
        splashing down as warmly as that
          natatorium long ago was chill.
      Later that year, I stood by the wall
  along the River Arno with sweet Victoria,
         hand in hand above the ancient
          stream, wrapping stories of our
unfolding around each other. The summer
brought us home to America, each to a different
   coast. The stories stretched but held.

  Over the next two years, we kept exchanging
      sheaves of typescript, hoping some day
        to be separated by less than paper.
         But her voice, which seemed to me
    as pure and bright as silver, darkened; worse,
          it rang false notes. I told her so.
Her mom caught her blushing, reading my letter, she wrote.
    Just then, when we were closer than paper,
   a person took a telephone call and told me,
      "I'm sorry, Vicky's died in a car crash."

    Perhaps it was merely to reassure myself
       how unexceptional my desires
that now my mind replaced my surroundings with

her face, in which feelings glinted and shimmered
like the hues in an opal, her willowy body,
breasts I never held except
against my chest, her breath, all that I carry
as if never pulled from a smoldering
wreck, smoldering still, offered, accepted, and
torn – but not wholly – away. The only

choice that love allows is whether to be
open to it; when we let it,
love sees with our eyes; but when our eyes see
what love sees, they blink; except for
that one photographic flash, it's gone.
And now I remembered Matthew Shepard,
beaten and tied to that fence in Wyoming's night,
and knew that Vicky had been my bridge
to where I was right now, this place of loss
in which all losses are united.

Soon I was treading on a trail of my tears,
dark grey dots on lighter grey.
"*Voi! Siete fiorentini?*" Dante
hollered. At that, I had to look up.
About as far away as his voice might reach,
columns of orange and gold-flecked light
danced across the dismal, sandy waste.
Widely scattered, other bunches
shot towards the horizon. They looked like searchlights,
aiming up. Moving closer,

the troupe that Dante'd hailed revealed that something
dark at each column's base was a person.
I watched a flake of soot drift over one.
Passing overhead, it kindled,
drifted down and settled blazing to his
shoulder. He frantically brushed it off,
flailing his arms and jerking his body. The beam of
light above him widened and narrowed
to match his movements. Mostly they waved their arms
at the sky, and this contributed to

the semblance of dancing. It might have seemed sacred and joyful
but for the fires they batted away.
Every ash that floated above them flared into
incandescence and fell upon them.
As we moved closer, the illusion that their
bodies projected solid rays of
light dissolved, and they resembled insects
caught beneath lamps on a summer night.
Soon, they were near enough to speak to Dante.
"No Italians here, my brother,"

said a man. He eyed me. "That one still
fills out his form." Dante explained,
then said, "But I accosted you to know,
do you have news of Brunetto Latini?"
"Nothing recent," said the man, "Years ago, he
fell from the grace that we have found here

Praise Christ Jesus and the chaste life!"
Like a conductor, he led the others:
"Love the sinner! Hate the sin!" they chanted,
circling beneath us. Dante said,

"It gladdens me to hear that he is fled.
Whatever pains he now endures
are surely not self-hatred." To me, he said,
"Come. There's nothing more to learn."
"No, stay! And join our praise of the chastened spirit!"
The man raised his arms, then threw them around
my ankle. Kicking, my foot flew over his head.
An ember grazed my heel. The shock
burned up my calf and thigh, across my groin
and to the tip of my cock. I gasped.

Dante hauled me away and held my elbow
until I could walk by myself, explaining,
"Here are those who cannot abide the object
their love has chosen. You have a saying,
uncomfortable in one's skin? That may describe them."
"You wrote that you found the sodomites here."
"I never meant that men are baked for loving
men. Those I saw here used boys; they
flash their wands upstairs now, with the priests.
I did not see Brunetto among them."

Canto XVI

Ahead we heard a distant, steady rumbling,
as if the desert, emerged from that dreadful
pulsing surf, would end in unremitting
noise. Our pace deliberate, my
guide restrained his urge to hurry more than
my recovering strength would permit.
We spoke of Brunetto Latini, that friend and mentor
whom Dante credited even in hell
with teaching him the means of immortality:
to write of love in everyone's tongue.

I said, "I understand your fondness for his
writings. They showed you your way. But after
what he did, to hold him in such affection…"
"I saw him suffer a judgment greater
than any I could render, this man who gave me
the keys to escape the solitary
confinement that is life without expression.
Every touch to him was fire.
If it was not the touch he desired, it burned him
as sorely as if it were. Witnessing

how, while bearing such scars, he held himself in the
grace and esteem of all who knew him,
I forgave the use he'd made of me, so
small to me, so painful for him, so
long ago." He sighed. We walked in silence.
"But how could you forgive what your god
so awfully couldn't?" I pressed. "My will was not yet
tuned to the true pitch," he said,
"or so I might have answered seven hundred
years ago. But you may take god

out of it. I had not yet looked into eyes –
and seen myself reflected in them,
as your Victoria will show you! – that love not
what is false. I hadn't forgotten the
feeling of sin, and with it that peculiarly
limited compassion which softens to others'
pain when it reminds us of our own."
Something in the depths of his
ambivalence extended a tendril into me,
carrying, like a hand that offers a

delicate china cup of tea, a vision:
myself, exposed and unable to hide
in abyssal radiant blue. I sipped, so to speak,
and pondered while he pointed out
the unforgiven, clustered hither and yon,
like to like, illuminating –
fiercely! – only themselves in the dreary landscape,

the ones repelled by the shapes of their love.
I thought I saw someone I knew among them, but
I held back so as not to disturb her.

We came to a troupe of twelve or thirteen, circling,
hands upon each other's shoulders
like folk dancers, just beside our highway, their
twinkling columns merged into a
tube around a core of dingy dimness,
into which they faced. "Hello,"
one called to us. "I overheard you talking.
Tell me, please: are you an American?"
He pronounced it "Amurrkin." "Yes," I said.
"Glory," he said, "a creature of flesh,

still in it! And here you are, scuffling our pavement
so even the dead can hear! Excuse
me asking a personal question, but how in heaven's
name did you swing that?" Dante
answered for me: "The Beloved calls him,
to take the long road back to Her."
You could hear the capitol "B" in "Beloved,"
the way he said it. Our interlocutor
jerked his head at that, from disbelief
or surprise, perhaps; perhaps to flick

with his long hair a flaring ember off his
shoulder. All their heads were twitching, as
active as horses' tails in horsefly season.

"Tell me, friend," he said to me,
"do family values and traditional marriage
survive in the heartland?" "All too well,"
I answered. "I take it you call yourself a Christian?"
"Like all of our little congregation."
He had the charm of someone who assumes
that you are his brother in salvation,

until he discovers you're not. Then it hardens
like obsidian, edge chipped sharp to the
same degree he figures you are fallen.
"Sinners reborn to the Lord," he said,
and savored the "L." His head switched back and forth,
sending his locks streaming against a
flurry of flames descending towards him. The stink of
burning hair rose to us. "And you,
my boy? Have you accepted your personal saviour?"
Dante again to the rescue: "Not

in such a way that someone like you would recognize."
He pulled me by the elbow. "Come.
We've far to go and nothing to learn from these."
But as we walked away, the pastor
yelled, "Don't be so all-fired high and mighty –
pride goeth before a fall.
Did I tell you that our flock is small?
It's growing daily! Soon, we'll call
our own your Representative Robert Dornan,
and the lady who crushed the fruits

infesting her Florida sunshine tree, and the lord be
praised! the reverend who spreads the word that
god hates fags..." "He's not my rep!" I hollered,
"I'm a Vermonter and damn proud of it!"
"Vermont?!" he cried, "Tell Nancy Sheltra that we
wait for her with open arms!
We'll make a ring around the world! And marry
it to god!" Their dance grew frenzied.
Their eyes rolled wildly. They flung their heads with abandon.
Their shoulders heaved. But from the navel

down, they shuffled stiffly, a carousel of
tight-clenched buttocks engirdling nothing.
"How can they not know just where they are?"
I asked my guide. "Oh, but they do,"
he answered. "As in life, so in death.
Their fatal mistake has ever been
their faith that they are in it but not of it."
Shortly further on, the roaring
swallowed whatever ejaculations of praise or
vituperation they might have flung,

although I still could faintly see them revolving
their empty axis, as we
stood on the brink of the last pit. The stream
tossed rusty gouts to invisible depths.
They seemed to fall slowly, shivering into spray
and cacophony welling up against them.

The far side of the circular escarpment was lost
in the mists this huge, vague maw exhaled.
The smells and sounds were equal in loudness. Recoiling,
we turned together and bowed our heads

the way people do in bars when they want to talk
and the band is playing. He had me search
my pockets until I found a crumpled portrait
of him who could not tell a lie.
Shouting instructions in my ear, he had me
spread it carefully across my knee,
uncrease it, smooth it until no line could be seen
to furrow that candid, dome-like brow,
fold it into a little paper airplane, and
send it spiralling down the deep.

Canto XVII

It corkscrewed down like a Fokker Fellowship
evading fire at Baghdad Airport.
Standing on the brink of all that sheer
hollow, watching my tiny glider
gradually vanish within, I strained to
see, swimming through the air
upwards at us, that monster, Geryon, Dante
had reported met him and his
guide here, with the head and shoulders of a
charming man, a serpent's brilliantly

patterned body, and a scorpion's tapering,
deadly tail. Virgil seated
amidships to shield him, Dante had ridden the beast
a gyring flight to the bottom, or so
he averred. But you, dear reader, will have to weigh
his credibility for yourself.
We waited and waited. Nothing swarmed up at us,
unless you count the steadily welling,
noxious mists, like nothingness made visible.
"You should go and talk to those people,"

said Dante. "I'll call you when it comes. Stay near."
His voice conveyed a suave irritation,
like a tour guide when, unexpectedly,
the museums are closed. "Okay,"
I said. The souls to whom he directed me
were squatting in groups of three or four
along the granite lip that held the sands
from flowing over the precipice.
Their bodies were blackened with grime. I kept to the rim,
where the soot didn't fall. As I approached,

I saw that they were busy with little plastic
spades and buckets, red and blue and
green and yellow, battered as toys are after a
season at the beach. "Well, looky,"
one greeted me, "a living, breathing white boy.
You looking for some kind of action,
honey?" She straightened her back and smiled at me.
Her eyes were dead. Momentarily
at a loss for how to answer, I stole a
page from Dante's book. "Tell me

who you are and I will say your name to
those to whom your name still counts."
"Name? Don't nobody give a shit about that.
But if you want to know, I'll give
you what you want for free, 'cause you so pretty.
I was a bag lady for the numbers
up in Harlem. Brought a big man down

for sayin' so, but it was true,
hee hee! Don't nobody mess with me."
She'd turned to me to talk, and the man

to whom she'd turned her back was inching his hand
towards her bucket. As if to prove
her point, she clapped her right hand on his wrist
and flung it at him, all without taking
those expressionless eyes off me. He swung his
fist, with its pale bracelet where her
fingers had smudged the grime, but missed, and kicking
back to balance himself, he scattered
the mound to which his right-hand neighbor was adding
scoops of sand, at which that worthy

hurled away his implements and fell on
the offending leg, biting.
So they went at it. Over their bestial noises, she
said, still smiling, "Now, that thieving
sack of turds, in case you want to know, was
mister big time, back in the sunlight. He'd
borrow a lot of money and buy a business,
then he'd strip it. Like a car.
Unload that back seat, it just weigh us down,
and we don't need no hub caps, neither.

Sell them. Then he'd drive it fast and far as
it could go without no oil, and
slap some paint and bondo onto it and

find a sucker who'd think there was anything
left for him to squeeze from it. You know
what I'm saying? They called him a wizard on Wall Street.
And my friend who's snacking on him, he was a
international development banker."
She pronounced it slowly, with pride. The banker
lifted his head and, jamming his hand

beneath the raider's chin as if to shove it
through his forehead, sighed and said,
"My dear, I thank you for whatever words you
kindly were about to utter,
but I fear my principals might not
appreciate a public statement
of our connection at this time." Savagely
twisting his neck, the raider caught the
web of the banker's thumb in his teeth, and worried it.
The banker howled and was released.

The raider growled, "Tell him who your pal
here loaned his money to, and what they bought,
and who were the sorry shits who paid him back."
"I think I can guess," I said, "and I'm certain
the bantus were glad to service the interest on
the guns the government used to shoot them."
"That was another firm, not mine. Our projects were
strictly legitimate. Dams and airports,
and such." "I have no doubt that they were needed
just as much as schools and clinics.

But what's his story?" I pointed at the fourth,
a paunchy, balding man, who sat
a little apart, contemplating the sand
between his legs. With baggy eyes
he gazed at me, then mournfully said, "I don't
know what I'm doing with these people.
I ran a chain of rent-to-owns. Maybe
you saw our ads. Big Al, they called me."
"Sure, I saw them, you crazy motherfucker,"
interjected the bag lady, her mouth

now straight and grim. "And what you didn't tell
the brothers and sisters was how many times
they had to pay what those broke-down couches and busted
teevees was worth before they owned them.
But of course by then you'd took them back
because they was a month behind."
At that, their buckets became artillery, and I,
to avoid becoming collateral damage,
left them bailing as fast as they could, and returned
to where my leader pensively gazed

upon the void. "So, where is Geryon?" I asked.
"The one whose stench afflicts the world,
as I described him, is not like the monsters
you have seen so far – caged, or
slain, or superceded – or like the demons –
evolved into terrors beyond your conscious

recognition. The beast *con la coda aguzza,*
che passa i monti e rompe i muri
e l'armi, who hid his sting behind a
show of justice in my day, in

yours acknowledged king of kings, has grown
beyond transporting the likes of us,
and this, which was his kennel, is now his toilet.
I'd heard an elevator was
installed here, manned by one of Geryon's offspring.
He's said to wear a uniform,
a crimson coat with lots of gold embroidery.
But the summons I was taught seems
not to work. Perhaps it's out of order."
So he answered, sighing, "This is

not the first time I have been misled.
However, I know another way;
a hard one, to be sure. Please follow me."
He showed me to a staircase built
of railroad ties sunk in the living rock
and wending down until they looked
like toothpicks, then like hairs, and then were gone
beyond where sight could follow them.
No banister hemmed us in. Upon each beam,
which groaned as if about to break

when I confided my weight to it, was carved
a name: *Bernie Cornfeld; Lou "The Fixer"*

Blunger; Tino De Angelis; Susanna Hill;
the man who sold the Eiffel Tower;
Carlo Ponzi; William Thompson; Gregor
MacGregor, Cazique of Poyais; and last,
a stubby step completing descent from the realm of malice
to the realm of fraud, stubby,
as if it had yet to fully grow into place,
the fresh-cut legend "AHMED CHALABI."

Canto XVIII

As soon as our feet hit the rock, a roiling hubbub
enveloped us, like when, emerging
from the concrete bowels of one of our major
sportspalasten, from the fusty
halls of beer, popcorn, and trough-shaped urinals
through a tunnel darkened by contrast
with the light at its end, opens around you the
populated bowl, its tens of
thousands of voices all converging upon you.
Underlying this, the waterfall's

distant roar, as steady as urban traffic.
But where was the clamoring mob? Visible
only the iron-colored granite floor of the
vast amphitheatre. Then,
I remembered. Dante had mapped here trenches, nested
concentrically, surrounding a central well,
a different species of suffering filling each,
beneath one's line of sight until
one came upon them. Yet another question
nagged me: "Chalabhi? I know that name.

A fraudster, wanted in Jordan. But he's not dead!"
My leader halted and lowered his lips
to my approaching ears. "You keep on thinking
this is all some <u>final</u> judgment.
A man who buys a cemetery plot
has both his feet in the grave, but he walks.
It's nothing more mystical than that. Now, come here."
He led me up some shallow ledges that
could have been crudely fashioned stairs onto a
spur that jutted, bridge-like, over a

busily echoing channel. Now that we were
directly overhead, new sounds
were added to the ruckus: brushing, thudding,
the hordes of naked men below
rushed past and into one another, scurrying
willy-nilly. Also, they creaked.
"Their skin is thick as saddle leather," explained
my master, when I asked, and now
I knew that their features looked poorly molded and coarse
because they were, and not because

my vision was so impaired it could not distinguish
jowls from a commanding chin.
Often in spring, I've leaned on the rail of the bridge near the
ballpark in Waterbury, watching the
turbid Winooski slide by, trying to spot the first
fish of the season. Peering upstream
into this throng was much like that. I tried to

recognize someone, but it was useless.
My seeking eye could find no point of purchase
in the rapidly moving flow of

nearly monochromatic shades of tan that
merged into a river of many
braiding currents, and just as a face emerged to
near familiarity, it
faded into the masses, like a leaf
the springtime Winooski draws from its bottom,
boiling towards the surface, then withdraws.
Recalling then whom Dante'd found
consigned to this sad groove, I said to him,
"But surely there aren't pimps and seducers

enough in the world to make such a swollen river!"
"In my time, those were the recognized
violations men committed against those,
who, on god's behalf and imitating
him, give birth. But you – I mean, your age –
perceives more broadly what is flattened
when a man denies what's due to women.
The currents you see here, twining and blending
like a nest of snakes, all carry different
grades of formerly human silt: your

pimps and seducers, sure; as well, your porno
movie makers; ad execs who
swore by the creed, *sex sells*; your bosses who

bartered employment for blow jobs;
wife beaters; good old boys who kept 'the cunts' from
joining the clubs where the deals were made; the
chef who trained the waitress to know her station by
squeezing her tit with his tongs when she asked him
if her order was ready; your anti-abortion
crusaders who blocked the clinic's doors so the

scared young woman must carry their ranting urgency
with her like a seed of rape.
You know how my religion flows from my love
of a woman as from a clear spring.
Let us not linger here. These make me sick."
The span we crossed made one smooth arch
supported by half a dozen abutments, and as
we approached the last of these, a face
among the swarm below leaped into focus,
known to me. He caught my glance.

"Why are you looking at me? Move on!" he yelled.
"William? Is that you? Tell me,
what is your big hurry?" I yelled back.
"I'm looking for women. A man has his needs."
He lowered his head and dived back into obscurity.
Now our bridge descended to the
dike, as wide as the playing fields of Eton, but
stone instead of grass, that walled the
depression we'd just crossed from the next one down.
The dwindling clamor behind us mingled

with a swelling stink. We mounted the ramp to an
asymmetrical overpass,
higher at this end than at the other,
like where old Route 2 traverses
I-91 aslant, diving into
St. Johnsbury on what the locals
used to call "the banzai bridge." Beneath us,
a fug so thick my nose misled
my eyes to think the churning brown they saw
was but a cloud of noxious vapors

whose reeking arms reached up to embrace us. But no.
A longer look discerned the human
forms below. The stench snapped into focus.
The muck they wallowed in was shit.
"This pouch seems not changed much," my leader murmured.
"Oh, we cater to a whole new
clientele," responded a deep voice.
Unnoticed, its owner, a whirling blankness, had
joined us on the bridge. "But who?" asked Dante,
unfazed as ever. "Your flatterers, of course,

remain most loyal. Propagandists, at the
pricier tables. But lately we're swamped with
what I call the Devotees of Metonymy,
those who took their part of mankind
(love that word!) for the whole. You've seen *Casablanca*?
It's like my favorite scene, when the Germans

whoop it up at Rick's." But no one below was
carousing. No anthems rose to us, just
feculence. Then Dante: "Could you point out
someone a living Yankee might know ?"

"With pleasure," the oily voice replied. "That group
of three just there – that's Dr. Goebbels
enjoying tea with William Randolph Hearst
and William Loeb. Hey, Bill," it shouted,
"tell us what you remember about the *Maine*!"
I guess it was Hearst who raised his head,
but watching what extruded from his mouth
and plopped onto his chest undid me.
Retching and drooling, I staggered away in a hurry,
chased by the demon's mocking laughter.

Canto XIX

"Watch that one," my teacher whispered. "What?"
I asked, in normal tones, but before
my tongue had clapped my teeth, a sudden enormous
rustling drowned me out. It stopped a
second after I did. "Shush," he whispered,
"here we must speak *sotto voce*.
Look." Again he pointed upwards from the
bridge where we, midway across the third and
by far deepest ditch – a gorge as sheer and
abysmal as the Niagara River

cuts below the Falls – had paused. The noise had
issued from beneath us, so,
before obeying his injunction to raise my
eyes, I glanced back down, but nothing
but the turgid torrent, brownish
greenish untranslucent thickly roiling,
stirred in the depths, like what we'd seen elsewhere.
Where he pointed, one of the birds that
I called "carrier pigeons" was gliding towards us,
clutching someone dangling limply.

I had time to think that its paper wings, a
point on the flood directly beneath them, and
I formed an equilateral triangle when it
unburdened itself and bounded away like an
arrow, out of sight. Released, its cargo
disintegrated on the air
into a dully shimmering cloud, dispersing
slowly as it fell, a rain of
oblong confetti that drifted under our bridge.
One piece landed near me. Dante

nodding approval, I stooped to pick it up.
The face on the lozenge was not the face of the
man whose polestar had been what was honorable, but
otherwise it resembled a dollar.
I brought it over to Dante. "Ask," he whispered.
"Who," I breathed, but that was all.
The lines that formed the lips on the picture rippled
and words were heard. The sound, however,
exploded from far below us,
thunderous echoing blast of millions of voices.

They began with "we," and "power" followed
soon thereafter, but so reverberant
were the concatenating eruptions of noise,
the sense was altogether lost.
Thinking I had a clue, "What power?" I asked.
"King of kings!" the canyon rang
until the words dissolved in blurry uproar,

like a chorus in Handel's nightmares.
Dante motioned me to follow him and
led me to the end of the bridge,

then another hundred feet from the brink
into a hollow in the rock, just
big enough for two to crouch. A shallow
dolmen roofed this refuge. Dante
said, his vocal cords just barely vibrating,
"Here we may talk. Speak to him softly;
he has no power but to respond in kind.
Mere human voice is all that's left him,
removed from his friends." And when I looked around,
bewildered, Dante pointed at the

scrap of paper I still clutched in my hand.
I cleared my throat, then, "Who are you?"
I uttered, feeling foolish addressing a dollar,
but once again the tiny lips parted.
"I am nobody. I am what I gave myself
up to, tool and vehicle, just like
everyone who is dropped down here." The voice was
surprisingly mild and sad. "But what you
really want to know are the facts of my case.
I'll tell you those, if you agree to

reunite me with the rest when I'm done: but
I will name no names." "All right."
"I was professor of endocrinology at a

very prominent university,
director of a research lab and mentor to
numerous graduate students and junior
faculty, some of whom have distinguished careers.
Although first author of many papers
concerning widely varied topics, my specialty
was a disease – well, I won't tell you.

I'm proud to have been identified with it,
and that my work will some day help
to relieve a pretty fair amount of misery.
A pharmaceutical company funded
one of my larger studies, saw the promise,
engaged my services as a consultant.
Meanwhile, my work had made me known in circles
outside the academic sphere, and
I was recruited to serve on panels reviewing
the safety and efficacy of drugs.

How exciting they were, those commuter flights
to Reagan Airport to protect the public!
How important I felt my role to be!
Until that day our panel voted
on an application of my patron's,
and I sided with approval,
and the side effect was many deaths."
The voice grew smaller until I fancied
I was reading that engraving, not hearing it.
"Science," I said, "proceeds for the most part by

gradual accretion, like a coral reef, a
gigantic structure built of the tiny
accumulated efforts of generations
of interchangeable invertebrates.
Whatever you discovered was there before you
and might as well have been found by another.
So don't you talk to me of pride, you pathetic
whore; your pride is proof of your falsity.
I don't know who else this confetti parade is
made of, but I can guess: the public

relations flacks, the lawyers and lobbyists,
the think tank scholars whose expertise
so nicely supported whatever their sponsors wanted.
Also, reporters and editors who
followed the money (*pace* Woodward and Bernstein) —
they told us what the money wanted
us to know, and estimated the worth of
politicians by the size of their
campaign coffers. Political fundraisers, too, and
pitchmen for sale to the highest bidder;

what a crowd is devoted to making sure that
nothing is heard in the halls of power that
interferes with the right to make a buck! And
every one of them can point to some
orphan he patted on the head or little old
lady she could have run over but didn't.

William Penn said government is *a sacred
thing in its institutions and purpose*, but
he was an old-fashioned Quaker with a wig.
You want to be sent to join your soul-mates?

I wish I had a book of matches and all
of you in one big pile." And Dante
smiled while I wadded it between my palms
into the tightest ball I could. Then,
pinching it between my thumb and forefinger,
I walked back to the brink and yelled
uncaring into the thunder, "Let justice well up as
waters, righteousness like a mighty
stream!" and placed the ball between my lips
and spat it to the polluted river.

Canto XX

The fourth ditch was the first I found unchanged
    from the way my teacher had found it.
Below us shuffled a woeful procession of naked
    men and women, their heads twisted
one hundred eighty degrees around. Their buttocks
    preceded their hair-draped clavicles. I
can say that I saw several whose tears ran down
    between their butt-cheeks, as Dante'd reported.
"Maestro," I started to say, but he hushed me.
    "There's something that I missed," he said,

and then I saw it, too: their eyes were rotated
    inwards as if they strained to see
ahead through their skulls, and that was horrible
    to me in a way the screwed-up necks,
so merely grotesque, were not. Blind and mute, on
    sibilant feet they crept along.
"Looking down from above, and it's so dim…"
I offered, but he wouldn't have it. "Like chickens,"
he said, "That's what I thought when I first saw
    them. Wrung for the pot. An image I

could use to hold at bay, for a moment, the ice
that invaded my stomach. You know I studied
the stars. My life had brought me one short step
from marching here, among the soothsayers!
Soon as I realized that, the stupid image
dissolved, and I unfroze, and wept.
It blurred my vision." "Nothing's seen clearly, in hell,"
I offered again. This time he smiled.
"Hell, as someone wrote – was it Thomas Hobbes?
I'll ask him – is truth seen too late.

But your compassion, for which I thank you, is
misplaced. I have reached that state
of relaxation, beyond your little tenses,
where all my perceptions are perfectly timely.
So are yours, if only you could know it.
One winds up here by feigning to see
the truth too soon. *Sub specie aeternatis*,
that is the same as seeing it never.
Outside this moment are no visible truths,
only possibilities and

the detritus they leave once they have struck
the wafer-thin adamant moving through time
that you call existence. The ones who shuffle down there
in the trench predicted elections,
told you what the President would say
before he'd said it, announced what color
everyone would wear next season, directed

your fears to the next big threat, and drove
phantasms into millions of brainpans, like spikes –
dreadfully deadening. If you know what the

President will say, you do not listen to
what he says. If you know what
color to wear, the rainbow collapses. If you
fear what they tell you to fear, the knife will
find you from the darkest corner." He paused,
as if to collect his thoughts. I said,
"I know that history teaches illusions can kill.
Just such unreality can lead to
vernichtung. But you seem to go beyond that, I think,
by talking of possibility.

So tell me, how can one annihilate
what doesn't exist to begin with?" He said,
"To answer that requires a shift of perspective.
Filtered through your senses, which number
more than five, and screened by your preconceptions,
emotions, desires, cognition, and habits,
a fluctuating pattern of interference
created by coruscating beams
of *maybe*, *perhaps* and *probably* refracting
and criss-crossing fills your sky with

stars, proposes the earth and your feet to walk there,
holographically frames your experience,
outside which is nothing you can know.

Those you see below us, sliding
in that groove, as captive as phonograph needles,
denied whole worlds that might have been
when they diverted attention from what is
to their impoverished, partial visions.
By that, they damaged the fabric of which themselves
and everything else in the world is woven."

I might have asked so many questions I couldn't
settle on one, but let them flow
through me until he said, "That fellow, there,
with olive skin, the one whose head
is bowed to where his shoulder blades might pinch
his nose, I know him! And his life
might illustrate the point in yet a third way.
In the flesh, he walked the sun-bleached
hills and groves of Greece. The way I heard it,
in his manhood's youth he chanced

upon a pair of giant serpents, entwined
and copulating, blocking his path.
The sight of it emptied his mind of all but wonder
and disgust. Eventually, thoughts of
where he wanted to go came creeping back in.
To kill or drive them away, he whacked
the nearest one, the female, with a stick.
Some say he injured her, but pain,
perhaps, as your law of simple assault sets forth,
was injury enough; upon which,

he changed into a woman. I have not heard
the transformation described, and as
you see, he does not speak. The proof is this:
she bore three children. Seven years:
the serpents once again lay in her path,
and once again she struck the nearest.
Why she did is not so simple. Perhaps
some day you'll write about it. This time,
she struck the male; whereupon, her daughters
lost their mother and gained a father.

Not long later, he was called to compare a
man's and a woman's pleasure of loving.
Of ten parts, a man enjoys but one;
a woman enjoys all ten in her heart,
was his reply, and with it he knew his blindness.
Often when a sense is lost its
animating force takes refuge in
another faculty, doubling its strength.
So with Tiresias. Missing full sight of the present, he
dourly told of future things."

"That doesn't sound so hellish," I said. The rebuke
came quickly. "Use your mind. Knowingly –
bitterly! – drowning his sense of the whole in his sense of
compensated loss, he traded the
ocean and all its salty skies he held
within for a set of monorail tracks.

If that is not offensive to god, what is?"
"If you mean he's fundamentally
miserable, I guess I have to agree," I said.
He answered, "And the lives he trammeled

with his words, that squeezed them into a car
like refugees speeding from uncertainty?
Menoeceus? You don't know that story?
You could look it up. For him,
it was a cattle car, conveying to slaughter.
But let me bring it closer to you.
There's Tiresias' daughter, Manto, a famous
seer, watering her sternward cleavage.
Until not long ago she lingered in limbo.
Oh, she tracked this slot as well:

we dead are everywhere our lives brought us.
In that, we most resemble the living.
Among the pagans, she was known for virtue.
So she enjoyed the friendship of Virgil,
Aristotle, Gilgamesh, Confucius,
Murasaki Shikibu,
and all that hopeless intelligent *menschlekhkeyt* – "
he slyly shot me a smile, as if
we shared a joke – "until their liberation,
when the insurmountable wall

of faith no longer stood between them and their joy.
Then she was freed to re-enter the world,

and with her table-rapping, crystal-gazing,
tea-leaf-reading, prognosticating of
every stripe gained currency, until
you can't tell news from vaporous figments.
Yes, there truly is a spirit of prophecy,
known to those who swim in the ocean and
feel its currents, but that is lost to you and
counterfeit here. Let's move along."

Canto XXI

Remember that package of pork ribs you brought home
the day it was marked for expiration?
You slid it onto the shelf beneath the drawer
in which you keep the cheeses and cold
cuts, meaning to grill tomorrow, but it rained.
It rained the next two days, and then you
forgot the ribs for a few days more. Remember what
blossomed forth when you pierced the shrink wrap?
That scent, blended with undertones of urine
and diarrhea's rounded sourness,

filled the ditch we came to now, and greeted
us before we reached its lip.
Within, the sources of the stench sat slumped
in rows of wheelchairs facing outwards
to the iron-colored walls, much like the
residents of a nursing home I'd
visited several decades ago, who'd lined both
sides of a windowed hallway. But they'd been
positioned so that the things before their eyes
were each other, to whom their indifference

equaled that of those in the recreation
room to the snowy imbecility
of the ceiling-mounted television
they were parked beneath. These,
unlike those still awaiting death at L.A.'s
Veterans' Administration, reposed in
pools of their own filth and even from our
perch so many feet above the
oozing pressure sores that cratered legs and
buttocks sometimes to the bone were

nearly as plain to sight as the breath of their
decay was loud to smell. The bridge
across this gutter had collapsed. "How much
has changed. This arch still stood, and the ditch
was brimming with boiling pitch, my last trip here,"
said Dante. Down the debris we carefully
picked our way, and I moved all the more slowly
the closer we got to where it led.
Among them, halitosis added its note
to the foul olfactory cacophony.

The place was hot, as if the air conditioning
had been cut to save on costs, and
airless, like a building whose windows are locked
because the management won't buy screens
and doesn't want the inmates to escape.
Glancing over the ranks of gaunt,
hollow-eyed heads, I saw some movement far

away in both directions, fast
converging on us. Dante saw it, too.
He said, "Kneel down and keep from sight

until I've had a chance to deal with them.
This crew is rough and arrogant. They
gave Virgil and me a hard time coming through here."
I crouched and, as he further directed,
scurried away from where he remained alone
and hid at last among the time-servers
between whom and the sheer rock wall was nothing.
Somewhere to my right, the ruined
bridge – *I wish we'd made a run for it,*
I thought, although I knew they could swiftly

chase and pick us off the teetering rubble.
"Malacoda," yelled my leader,
sounding less assured than I'd have liked,
"we meet again, but this time I
don't need to ask your help to find my way."
The answering voice was distant enough
that its harshly grating echoes obscured its sense,
at least to me, whose ears were shocked
immediately after by an intimate whisper.
"Hey, newcomer. What're ya in for?

Never mind. Don't talk. They catch you, strap you
down and it's all over. Don't you
worry, sonny, I won't squeal. Your little

secret's safe with me and my pals.
Your friend is fucked, though. The screws have got him good."
It may seem strange that I did not
look up to see the source of these words, but I
was frightened to raise my head, and the dirt
I fixed my eyes on was cleaner and less unpleasant
to view than any of those almost-

cadavers rotting around me. Malacoda
heard it, though, and roared, "Who's talking?"
Instant silence. Even the dead clammed up. Then,
voices like cans of gravel: "There!" "No,
it was that way!" "I'll teach him to keep his
pie hole shut!" "I'll rip him a new one!" And
louder, with oily inflections: "Don't I know you,
stranger? Where's your friend? I'd like a
little taste of him – or you." And Dante:
"You can't touch me, Scarmiglione."

Now a racket thick as steel wool. Fragments were
all that I made out of Dante's
firm, insistent monotone: "willed where
what is willed must be," was one, and
"as your colleagues up there learned," another.
"If that one we saw is just your
fellow tourist, why's he hiding?" demanded
Malacoda. "Barboniccia,
take Cagnazzo, Calcabrina, and
Ciriatto to the bridge," he ordered, "and

see that no one passes. Not even you, my
heavenly wop, are going to spring
one of my wards from here." At that, I almost
gave up hope, but faith in Dante
kept me on my knees. "Ah, Malacoda,
lording it over these fraudsters so long
has robbed you of any sense of the truth, not even
if it bit you on that musical
ass of yours," my leader said, "though even when
fewer scam artists clogged this sewer,

you were dim enough. So I will put it in
terms of the kind that you are used to.
Do you know William Crawfield? He is yet a
countryman of my companion's."
"See? I told you!" interrupted a voice like
boulders grinding. "Draghignazzo,
shut your yap!" commanded Malacoda.
Then, to Dante: "Sure, we know him.
Got a place reserved for him about half
way around the circle, near the

tar pits where your buddy might find us stewing
lots of his homeboys: Senator Williams and
Representative Thompson, for starters; and Kelly
will make a big splash soon, and all the
others who fell for that fake sheikh in Abscam.
We've already got the excavators

      opening pits for the Duke of San Diego
        and his leader, Tom the Hammer.
Your boy William won't swim with them. He grifted the
          hard way: just a private joe,

   betraying only the trust he'd earned, not like
     some House Majority Leader, say, whose
  spotty butt's gold-plated the day he's elected.
      Good enough to earn a seat here
with a real nice view, though, your slick Will. A
        buddy of your buddy, is he?
We'll save a place right next to your pal for him,
    and you can visit whenever you want."
   And Dante failed so long to respond to this,
     I knew what I had to do, and stood up.

Canto XXII

"I am his friend. And if you accuse me of being
worthy of your tender care, well,
let me tell you how I know that man whose
name my comrade mentioned, who still, so
far as I know, compresses New England soil
beneath his heels." I had their attention.
"He'll be here in a year," said Malacoda.
"He might have come from anywhere,"
I said, "South Africa, New York, Australia
all hold traces of his trail.

I think he is a citizen of the world.
He came to Warringham, Vermont,
a town enfolded in mountains like an acorn
in a pocket handkerchief.
But there are children here who never gather
acorns. He is drawn to them. The
Diagnostic and Statistical Manual
paints for them a spectrum of
disorders; its rubrics are their secret names.
He is a man of secrets. So, he

settles in among their parents, and soon he
is the cheerful, trusted caregiver,
daily in their homes, attending, feeding,
bathing, clothing, exercising the
damaged offspring, the eccentric hubs their
lives revolve around off kilter.
The gratitude he earns is so intense
it feels at times like love, to them.
To him the kids are meat and bones and not
much different from their foolish parents.

Unhampered by the pain of empathy,
how easy it is to overcome
his mere disgust and the itch of impatience, to seem
efficient as if with gentle kindness;
he's *good with the kids* – the way a mover's good
who bandies your refrigerator
out your door without defacing your walls.
It all is aimed to gain their trust."
A whisper from my left: "Who is this guy?"
"Shut up. It could be anybody,"

mumbled back the carcass on my right.
I didn't miss a beat. "He thrives.
He learns they feel the usual small-town grievance
at being neglected by institutions
housed in more populous places. Perhaps he stokes it.
Later they'll say the idea came from
somewhere they're unsure of – to create

an organization all their own
whose first concern's the families it's composed of.
The Executive Director?

Guess who. So he plants himself astride this
machine he's built whose every part
is a cam that he may play against the others."
I paused for breath and looked at Dante.
He nodded, slightly. I found strength to continue:
"But what you want to know is how
I know him. Its funny; in the world above,
we talk about what damns us by
describing its effects, by circumlocutions.
Crime and punishment, sin and history,

forests that distract us from the trees.
I suspect down here you speak
more to the point and also much more bluntly.
Bear with me. I've met him only
once, to speak to, and all he said was lies.
He sat across a table from me,
lawyer beside him. I knew his scam, by then.
It hardly mattered what he said,
inviting our belief with such bland charm,
smiling and looking straight at me

as if of course misunderstandings happen.
The records, full of charmless figures,
betrayed his skimmings from the funding stream,

where and when he'd knelt by the bank and
dipped his bucket in. I didn't tell him,
then, I'd seen the mud on his knees.
Later, outside a courtroom, I met his wife.
She said, *You've got the wrong man.*
Her voice trembled. Something in it would not
declare itself to me outright,

but it was there and wanted to break free.
She hurried away before it could.
I don't remember if she stood by her man
the day he finally copped his plea.
Even then, he squirmed like a snake on a stick.
When the judge said, 'Is it true,
the dummy corporation, fake invoices,
broken promises?' he flicked his
tongue on either side of yes until the
deal we'd struck was almost lost,

then gave the judge his assent. How did I know him?
I was his prosecutor. If
my words to you have made us more akin,
give me my chair and strap me down.
I wrestled with him through negotiations,
sweated between jail and freedom,
dragged him to that final tiny foray
into the nimbus surrounding truth,
brought back a sack of gold for his angry victims.
We're comrades in arms, he and I.

He is that ragged urchin Auden sang of,
aimless and alone, and I...
I know his fear of being trapped and taken."
Emptied of words, my vision broadened
to behold on either side of Dante
looming over him what looked like
giant charcoal scribbles with medical scrubs
flung haphazardly upon them.
The biggest – scrawled in bold and angular strokes –
just to his right I took to be their

leader, Malacoda; to the left, a
round one, snarled as tumbleweed;
the others blurred as I whipped my head around to
see whose sudden whine behind me
cut the air like a nasal blade: "You *shit*!
You sack of shit! We hid you, snitch.
But you're not one of us, you're one of them!"
"Sedate him!" bellowed Malacoda.
Simultaneously, a thicket of arms
sprang around me, profusely sprouting

yellowed talons to snatch and hook and tear my
few remaining filthy rags and
scrape my skin. I froze. A bear may crash through
jack pines, snapping their skinny,
barring limbs. Rooted by that image,
I watched three parallel, coarse black lines

speed towards me like indelible markers tracing
routes on a map. Still I stood.
Three of Malacoda's henchmen shrank as
they unraveled to my feet, then

gathered there in a hulking wall of tangle.
Someone screamed, his arm caught in it.
"Madcap Rubicane, quick, the needle,"
growled a demon. The one it addressed
produced a syringe – the kind that's used to inject
brine into hams – and plunged it into
the nearest wheelchair-bound belly. It seemed to stir,
the way a spoon may stir a sauce
or maybe the agonized muscles it stuck in
tugged the sticker around. That second,

I was plucked up by Dante, who easily flung me
across his shoulders and thus I floated
over the outstretched emaciated arms.
They held him back no more than wind
that's combed by fields of cornstalks in November
is blocked from hitting the side of the barn.
So he reached the pile of rubble and up it
rapidly swept. We paused at the brink.
And there enough of my wits caught up with me
to wonder why we were not blocked

by Malacoda's troops, and Dante whispered,
"They left their posts to quell the riot,"

and only later did it seem strange, for only
wordless gasps had left my lips,
mingling with the gasps and shrieks from below.
Dante's shoulders, steady as stone,
accepted my weight until my trembling stopped.
Then he offered a hand like a stirrup
for me to clamber down and rejoin the pit
of my stomach, and then we hurried on.

Canto XXIII

At length, we sauntered downhill side by side,
and I'd have enjoyed the cooler air
up here but that it carried an oily reek
I was not used to. The slope was gentle,
the surface hard and jarring knees and ankles,
so I was grateful our pace was slower,
the more so for Dante's reassurance my fears
a posse might follow us were misplaced.
"Like the rains, the stinks, the other miseries
suffered here, those balls of terror

stick with those whose affliction's their *ragion d'essere*.
They'd never come this far, my son,
even if not otherwise engaged."
The aural evidence of their engagement
had decrescendoed to a deniable level
for quite some distance now, but news
of it still spiked my eardrums from time to time.
"I cannot muster *schadenfreud*
enough," I said, "to be thankful for that distraction."
I thought that he, who'd booted the helpless

damned in the head with glee, might chide me now for
bleeding-hearted liberalism.
He said, "Are you the one who wrote, of that day
the airplanes crashed the twin towers,
*may those who planned this be devoured by those
who would devour them*, and also wished
that *those who would devour them may choke on it?*
Such balance would have served you well
in that intensive care ward. Now you know
(excuse the phrase) god's broken heart."

And since his words were not mere rhetoric,
they freed me to cry. When I was done,
I said, "I get it, now: how you could kick
that soul, and why I should have run."
"Those are the choices that hell presents to you; so
hell is hateful; and fellow feeling
degrades itself – for lack of a suitable object –
to paralyzingly painful pity,"
concurred my master. We walked in sober silence
until our toes were touching the edge

of the next ditch, the one where Dante, guided by Virgil,
had found the hypocrites in creeping
droves, encumbered by cloaks of gilded dross.
But airy and empty opened before us.
The former confining channel had been quarried
seventy acres square, ten stories
deep. A hanging valley notched the wall at

either end. Opposite us,
halfway up the ragged excavation,
a crew of half a dozen tiny

human figures on a ledge compelled
attention with the only motion
in all that dust-hued desolation, working –
or so it seemed from where we stood –
to expand it. Faintly, clicking and buzzing
reached across the space from them to us, the
clicking rhythmically related to their
jerking movements, the buzzing steady, but
more could not be discerned from such a distance.
An earthen ramp precipitously

dropped from our right to the bottom of the pit.
Another rose by the distant workers.
Our way was clear. We scrambled down and slid,
at cost to my knees and ankles. Crossing
the middle of the vast dugout, I had
the strangest sensation as if I heard
on either side bagpipe bands from afar,
just barely audible. I noticed
how each laboring figure – now above us –
struck the cliff with hammer and chisel and

instantly recoiled to the end of a tether, then
drew himself back by his rope, pausing
several times to kiss his own wrist, it seemed,

before attacking the rock face again.
"What –" I began, but "Wait," said my guide, "until we
reach them, and all will be explained."
And sure, as soon as we stepped off the treacherous,
crumbly slope onto the ledge
among them, it became clear, as I had suspected
increasingly strongly, their unceasing

kazoo chorus was made by wind out their backsides.
The man whose face is worth five cents –
which once upon a time would buy you something –
stood before me commanding the crew
with an air of graceful authority.
I looked at Dante. "Go ahead,"
he said. Before the patriarch could whack
the rock and bounce away, I cleared
my throat and whispered, "Mr. President?
Whatever are you doing here?"

"Your voice betrays you, sir – an American!
Permit me to introduce my colleagues,
among whom you will recognize a quartet
of our compatriots: William
Bullein Johnson, who stood up for the rights of
slaveholders to serve as missionaries
of his Christian faith on the basis, he said, of the
priesthood of all believers; the Reverend
J.H. Jackson, his negro brother in spirit,
who clung to power by savage means

among the powerless, maintaining his church's
meekness at least with respect to whites;
the other two, to judge by your age, already
are well known to you; and our sixth,
that twelfth among the pious Bishops of Rome,
who sought to secure his apostolic
holy and universal See, so called,
by keeping quiet about the Nazis'
injustice towards the children of Jesus' people.
Having long ago thrown off those

burdens that restrained this circle's citizens,
we dig for the legions yet undead
a space where they will wander free of crowding."
I took this politician's answer
for what it was worth. But what I have not captured
for you, dear reader, is the peculiar,
halting rhythm imparted to his speech by his
frequent pauses to press his lips to a
seeming wart or nipple on his right wrist,
puffing his cheeks, with a wheezing sound:

"we *hwee* dig for the legions yet undead a space *hwee*
where they will wander free of *hwee* crowding."
It strikingly harmonized the anal continuo.
"Why are you doing that?" I asked.
The answer, however, came from Dante: "As
in life the words they gave their public

being were merely shapes of air, so now the
denizens of this trench are bladders
containing lungs from which they must replenish
their substance, continuously leaking."

"Ingenious, is it not?" the Virginian commented.
"This small protuberance," he added,
"like the valve through which you inflate your bicycle
tires, affords us freedom of motion
and avoids that unpleasant flaccid condition,
unbearably tedious, in which we are
reduced to helpless respiratory chambers,
exposed to the whims of all and sundry
until the goodness of our fellows moves one
to lend his animating breath."

"And wouldn't you say that might be a very long time,
Mr. President?" The prissy mouth
that uttered these words belonged to a face I knew.
Rounded as a weathered brick,
mashed nose and dome-like forehead and baleful eyes
turned my way when I greeted him,
"Mr. Director Hoover! Democracy's secret
policeman. What a pleasant surprise
to find you here! I'd thought you were boxed up with
Dzerzhinski and that gang, or maybe

dancing barefoot with the closet queens."
"You'll find me wherever you turn, young man.

I contain multitudes." He gestured
expansively, as if to say
some day, my son, all this could be yours, and
as his hand's arc reached its outward
apogee, a figure that had been obscured
behind him bent obsequiously
forward and met it with his buck-toothed mouth –
"Hwee! Hwee! Hwee! Hwee!"

Canto XXIV

"Thank you, Mr. Attorney General."
It called to mind the scene in the movie
where diffident guests show Don Corleone respect
by nervously, fervently kissing his ring.
Even Jefferson seemed to withdraw into watchful
silence, like a *consigliere*.
But Bobby Kennedy broke the spell: "I thought
I might remind you, Mr. Director,
that some of us watch out for each other down here."
I caught the pain in his voice, and marveled

how deep it ran, and how he strangled it.
"Like the way you helped me watch out
for that communist degenerate
the negro King you liked so much,
you and your philandering brother – well, it
has enabled us to continue
our friendly collaboration, hasn't it?"
I don't think it was I alone
who saw the Director's mouth curl mockingly,
for Kennedy said, "Oh yes, but what

I should have done back in that life we shared
I can do now," and with his chisel
slashed that pug-face cheek to cheek: the nose
flapped up from stale air rushing out,
and soon Director Hoover had shrunk to a pulsating,
lung-shaped sac. "Until it heals,
no point in puffing him back up.
Anyone for a match of football? I love your
modern games," said Jefferson, hopefully.
Then, speaking to me: "Allow me to

address your evident shock, my friend. Those two
are ever at each other, like children
with pigs' bladders, whanging away. Bobby
would like to water liberty's tree,
only there's no blood to do it with, ha
ha! Edgar is... well... Edgar.
Fancied himself a junior Walsingham,
poor man, and can't forgive our Bobby
for seeing through it. *Video et taceo*, indeed!"
But Kennedy still was looking at me.

"I can't tell you," he said, "how I hate for
you to see me in this place.
Every time we turn our heads the other
way when we see the law flouted –
when we tolerate what we know to be wrong –
when we close our eyes and ears
to the corrupt because we are too busy,

or too frightened – when we fail to
speak up and speak out – we strike a blow
against freedom and decency

and justice. I said those words, and all those things
that I decried are what I did
when Mister Director Hoover asked me to,
and worse, I authorized his lawless
persecutions of those who sought no more
than freedom and decency and justice,
all for fear he'd turn his powerful knowledge
against my brother Jack instead
and cost us the power we were too afraid
to use, for all our talk of toughness.

And now tough-talking cowards fill the White House.
The thirty-fifth anniversary
of my assassination – shot by an Arab
who never could account for his motives –
will pass unnoticed three months after they
unleash an unprovoked war upon
an already suffering people. Their motives will never
be known. In their America,
the prophet Billmon will tell the few who listen,
Prostitutes pose as journalists

(or vice versa), Christian activists lobby
for legalized torture, generals swagger
like Rambo in front of the cameras but cringe before

their civilian masters in private, law
professors write secret memos justifying
creation of a police state,
sworn enemies of big government gorge
themselves on pork, vomit, then gorge
some more, while Senators with the racial
values of a klavern leader and

your president preach democracy by day,
by night rewrite the Geneva conventions,
and masquerade as compassionate conservatives."
"Why do you tell me these things?" I cried.
He said, "I could see from the way you panted you carried
some weight up the slope to here.
The President there would love to enlist you to pick
up a hammer and chisel, now wouldn't you, Tom?
He'd like to get a hand with some meat in it
to help with this project. But you're a tourist.

You'll be going back to the place where injustices
sing in choirs of pain and hope.
If you must report me to the living –
among these associates, digging this hole
for hordes whose future society does me no credit –
remember first and foremost my words
that chafed your sense of outrage until it was raw."
He sighed, and it seemed so extravagant,
a breath he could have used to hold himself up
expended into the space between us.

This gesture, more than anything else, appeared
to show he felt his situation
more than anyone I had met so far.
It took my speech away. I stared
at him, and he stared back, and nothing was
communicated: unlike an actor,
whose face and eyes convey fleet thoughts as subtly
as shifting shades of sunlight in water,
his visage hid behind itself. That sigh,
those words, discordant but almost congruent,

not to be resolved. Defeated, denied
even speculative communion,
I looked away and down, and feeling his eyes
upon me still, I somehow knew
my gesture tore at his helpless disappointment.
"Let us leave this contemptible crew.
We've far to go and *tempus fugit*": Dante's
voice as clear and fresh as water
called my attention back from the dust. "I'd rather
call them tragic," I answered, and moved my

feet back onto the steep and infirm ramp,
not stepping so much as cautiously sidling
across its loosely commingled quartzite chunks
the size of marbles, golfballs, and baseballs.
I hesitated. "Will I see you again?"
My eyes met his and this time saw

their fierceness and hunger give way to something else,
shuttered. He answered, "I don't know.
Once in this pit one can't see out of it."
Who first looked aside, I cannot tell.

It was a very slippery slope we ascended.
Too soft and slow a step risked not
compressing the stones enough to make them hold
once weight was shifted onto them,
but too emphatic a stride could dislodge them.
I labored to find the right footwork
so as not to ride a shower of scree
tumbling to the bottom. For Dante,
of course, it was no problem. At the top
I made him wait while my racing breathing

slowed to catch my breath. When the one was
close enough behind the other to
pass a baton, he said, "I see your country
has produced a form of government
my day did not know," and cocked an eyebrow
until together we brought out,
laughing, "Hypo-cracy!" "Though that was said of the
British first," I added. Below us,
on the pit's floor, the team had acceded to Jefferson's
wishes, and Bobby went out for a long one.

"How could Hoover know that he had entered
hell at many places, if Kennedy

told the truth?" I asked. My guru answered,
"They each were speaking of different elsewheres.
They look up where they stand and see themselves
reflected in the clouds, a dozen
images overlapping it might be,
one for each of their presences in this smog-bound
nest of pocks. But none can see beyond
his own, reflected, blurry face."

Canto XXV

At his order, fifty yards back there I'd
fallen belly down on the rock
behind the crest between the trenches, and wriggled
up the shale to here, "Head down, no
peeking over until I give the word.
The other side's the swale of thieves.
You don't want them to know you're here too soon."
Awaiting commands, then, I remembered:
The dust my rusty light blue Saab 96
kicked up from Addison County's dry

dirt roads hung back of me so dense I checked it
now and then in my rear view mirror,
just to see the trail I made, dun billows
bright in the treeless stretches; fields of
corn and cows, the Adirondacks blue and
distant, the Greens, well…midsummer green, the
empty seat beside me weighted with sun in the
treeless stretches, full of dancing
shadows when there were leaves to cast them, and all
along the drainage ditches barbed wire

    made good neighbors. I had been sent on a mission.
      Adrift a year out of college, I'd beached
    on that driest of strands, a lawyer's office, hired
     at poverty wages in lieu of the budget
      for a professional to investigate the
      stories our indigent clients told us,
    routinely lying. Just as routinely, despite
       our advice to take advantage of
     the humane fiction whereby innocence
      persists until it's otherwise proved –

that is, clam up – they spilled the beans to the cops,
       confessions they confided from a
      lack of confidence as many-layered and
      deep as the Appalachian rocks whose
    spurs, petering northwards to the plains of
       Quebec, they poorly dwelt among.
What vision of beauty guided this tenant was not
        apparent from the patch of dirt,
    an outgrown shoulder, I pulled to off the road
       and sat upon, my engine idling,

    half a minute while taking in the weathered
      clapboards, formerly painted red, and
     broken plastic children's toys, doorless
       refrigerator lying face up,
    coils of chicken wire, a dark green bag of
      styrofoam chunks, a stainy mattress,
    his life's random etcetera that littered the

weeds and grass his stoop, a sagging
board on cinder blocks, descended to.
I called through his screen door, and he came.

But not until the stoop creaks and we're almost
nose to nose across the screen does
unease vent its weary, suspicious "Yeah?"
"I'm from your lawyer, about the case.
I've got some papers for you to sign." Flattened
against the screen, the bona fides.
We're team mates, like in gym in high school, chosen
to sweat through a game we have to play
together although you'd rather hang out in
the boys' room, smoke and talk about girls.

Me, I'd do this even if they didn't
pay me, almost, which they almost
don't. Unlatched, the screen door slowly sighs
towards me. I back two steps down,
step two steps up, and reach behind to shut it.
A few steps in, he waits for me,
stoop-shouldered like some tall men, crew cut, silent,
by the cluttered kitchen table —
breakfast dishes, cereal box, a cup half
filled with coffee and a butt.

"I thought you were a girl," he says, but mildly;
almost intimate, this moment.
Mildly he moves the dishes to the sink

*with hardly any clatter,
mildly draws a chair back – tube frame, torn
nylon upholstery – sits and
mildly gazes at me, eye to eye
almost. My gosh, he's big. I fumble
papers, stoop to pick them off the floor,
give them to him to read, and ask him*

*while he's reading can I look out back?
Portentous unfamiliar words
engross him. "Sure," he mildly says. Back out, then,
clumsily dropping to the plank and
stumbling off it, screen door slamming shut,
I pick my way through the junk, around
the house's side into a maple's shade
that hasn't helped the scraggly rose bush
someone planted under the dryer vent,
emerging again into unveiled sunlight*

*that falls directly down upon an emerald
patch of grass so very gently
sloping to the water where the creek
extends an elbow at the house
no bank or muddy shore line intervening.
It's at its very fullest flood.
The ground is hard right down to where there's liquid
gleaming among the blades of grass.
A sheet the color of Sicilian olives
mirrors sun, the skinny birches*

*clumped inside the horseshoe curve a hundred
fifty feet away from me,
the long thick swath of graceful, unbroken stems
that bows above the almost
stagnant flow they stand within, the brilliant
damsel flies and drabber dragon
flies that flit and rest among them. Going
back inside, I saw he'd read the
papers, signed where he should sign. I thanked him,
gathered them, made for the door,*

*left him hunched at the table. I was halfway
to my car when his chair scraped the
linoleum, then slow footsteps, then, sadly,
"Whaddaya think my chances are?"
Unviolated reeds and tranquil waters
made it unlikely the boat they'd accused him of
stealing had floated innocently to his
backyard, as he'd claimed it did.
Turning to face him, I cheerily replied,
"Oh, that's for the lawyers to decide."*

*Our eyes met, his within the screened shade, mine
all drenched with light, but for one second
I felt the punch of a common understanding.
The shale had just about warmed to me.
So close and quiet my ear felt his words
as much as it heard them, my guide whispered,*

"Follow me when I run. I won't fool them for
long, so follow close. Keep running
straight ahead, whatever happens. Never
mind the boat, it has no bottom.

Run as fast as you can, and don't slow down."
As quick as smoke, he rose to his feet,
and waving his arms and yelling went over the top.
I lost a beat to surprise, then scrambled
to my knees, into a sprinter's crouch and
launched myself after. Like a snapshot,
what I saw is fixed in memory: a
lawn the length of a soccer field,
tilted gently downwards to a wetland
twice that width again, its slate-grey

surface sharply etched by cat-tails, grasses, and
drawn up on the shore, a wooden
dinghy's bottomless hull through which ferns grew.
Dante was about halfway there.
In northern Maine and Minnesota, I've seen
golden-brownish halos veil the
rumps and flanks of moose. Just so Dante,
and he matched the ruminants' stately
unconcern. The winged scourge swarmed off him and
hovered in my path – no time to

swerve – I hit them, they embraced me – from then,
visual memories are disjointed:

Dante, running knee-deep without splashing;
the nauseous bubbles that bellied my pant-leg
when the muck sucked the shoe off my right foot,
then my left; the black dots swarming.
They went for my eyes, invaded my nostrils and ears.
Their buzzing and humming drowned out my splashing.
Wherever my skin was exposed, they landed and bit,
crawling through my tangled hair to

welt my scalp, and penetrating to my
back and shoulders, chest and stomach
through my shirt, its rents and holes, and
thick on neck and face and arms,
injecting with each bite a bit of their substance to
thin out mine, and with this awful
addition I was forced to carry their stories –
I had no choice: their tiny itching
voices were under my skin, imperious selves,
inflammatory, in every tongue.

In all their multiplicity of mood
and personality, like the huge
and overwhelming drone their wings made,
so dense and intricate, but mindless,
so their voices obsessively converged
upon one common theme: their theft
of someone's labor, freedom, sexual being.
Under my skin, the mindless song of
slavers – hunters, traders, masters, drivers,

> black, white, red, and yellow.

It maddened me. And when I'd sloshed across,
and firm ground met my feet, and the water
inch by inch unveiled my legs to the onslaught of
unslaked swarms, I flailed my arms
against my body, bruising myself as I ran
and smashed the greedy swollen bodies
that covered me like teeth on a rasp, laughing
with rage to feel them crush and pop,
until a hot breeze drove away my pursuers
and I was coated in my own blood.

Canto XXVI

"You can't kill them," he said, "They're already dead.
The most you might have done for them
when they had living bodies would have been
to help recall their souls, so through
the pain of that rejoining they might redeem
themselves, like Washington, who freed
his slaves, or even your Mister Jefferson,
who retained at least the semblance
of humanity. For didn't he say
he trembled at the thought god might be

just and hoped some day emancipation would
spring from the masters' consent? The future
masters, of course. But now ? Well… let me rid you
of these loathsome remains. They hold no
terror for me." So, leaving me alone
upon that ridge top shivering in
disgust despite the hot gusts breathing from
the far side, Dante took my shirt
down to the creek and rinsed it, returned and tenderly
washed my smeared, encrusted skin, and

something in his touch was soothing as ointment.
When I was relaxed and nearly dry,
we set out again on the way we had to go.
Shortly before we reached the next ditch,
Dante told me he had restrained his gift for
vividness for the sake of precision
in describing it, for fear of misleading.
He wondered if his sacrifice had
brought someone closer to heaven. But I told him,
when we arrived, how it had cost me.

Though the place was just as he had found it,
it was not as I'd imagined.
*(Yes, he whispers as I write, but you
are far too sensuous, and your thought's
disorderly.)* It was the *fireflies*:
the striking image he'd started with –
while reining himself in – to evoke this dusky
trench that teems with crawling lights.
They illuminate themselves alone:
that was his point. A dozen might ring

around you, reader, and still this page would hide
its letters. But from his reportage,
one would picture peering into dark and
indeterminate depths a long way
down at distant brilliant specks. Instead, from a
shallowly parabolic bridge an
eighteen wheeler might just clear, we viewed a

milling mob of flames, each swollen
around the body that fueled it. They hissed
and threw up fringes of greasy smoke

we smelled as each one slowly passed beneath,
its blue tip sharp against the dimness.
"Here are the ones who emulated the serpent,
falsely advising. Your smudge pots,"
said Dante. He pointed to a conflagration
that seemed to flicker in syncopation.
"You!" he hollered, "heirs of Homer, come and
introduce your sorry selves!"
Like people pushing their way to the door of a crowded
subway car, sometimes sidling,

sometimes shoving, creating little eddies and
minor turbulence, they flowed to a
spot below us and not uncomfortably
bathed us in their hot breath.
Assembled at our feet, they fizzed and crackled
like snapping fingers, and then they sang :
"*Ooo-ooo-ooo shabba shabba shabba lang*
ooo-ooo-ooo ring-a lang wha-oh
da dum dum we praise love the highest love
young love as strong as stars above

taut stomachs and tight thighs and curly hair
soft light and lacy underwear
red roses long-stemmed glasses of red wine

*red boxes of choc'lates candles shine
the one you need that sweeps you off your feet
you need you need you need you need
ooo-ooo-ooo shabba shabba shabba lang
ooo-ooo-ooo ring-a lang wha-oh
da dum dum solve your problems soothe your cares
oh darling baby always there*

*you hug me kiss me hold me through the night
so I don't worry have no fright
with all your sweetness life is so complete
and so complete your sweetness sweet
I'd die if you decided not to meet
my need my need my need my need
ooo-ooo-ooo shabba shabba shabba lang
ooo-ooo-ooo ring-a lang wha-oh
da dum dum—*" Dante cut them off. "Enough!"
He glanced at me with disapproval.

It was so catchy, I'd been tapping my feet.
"You won't like that tune so much
when you hear it from the lips of one you
thought might finally be the one
whose heart could bear the terror and erosion,
boredom, irritation, naked
joy and hidden struggle adult love is
built on, day by day," he said.
That sobered me right up. "A prophecy!
Please tell me more," I said. And he:

"The good news is, she won't be singing it
about you." And while I mulled
the several ways this news might have been good,
my guide dismissed the melodic flames,
barking soldierly orders at others to come and
take their place. Concentric circles
filled the passway beneath our bridge, blocking
the random traffic to and fro.
"These are unlike any from my time,"
said Dante, his good humor restored.

Uniform and azure as the cones that
jet from gas burners turned on high,
they stood unwavering in beautiful
and perfect array, surrounding us
with seemingly blistering brilliance. Perhaps the blocks
of stone that held us in the air
above them shielded us, for I felt nothing,
not even a warmth on the soles of my feet,
although I should have been sizzling like a steak.
Suddenly, as if with one voice,

they chanted, "*We are going to get you hot
for all the things you have not got,*"
and I couldn't help but laugh. This time,
Dante's look was full of approval.
"Advertisers? Marketers?" I gasped.
He nodded. "Please, won't you shoo them away

before they get annoying," I asked, and he:
"Because you wish for what is good,
I cannot but fulfill it." And then he blew
upon them as a person blows

the candles on a birthday cake, but instead
of going out, they bowed and scattered.
"Wait here," he said, and leaped off the bridge as if
a drop of eighteen feet were nothing.
Dodging among the flames, he ran to one
much bigger than the rest, and after
animated conversation with it –
much waving of arms and body language –
the two of them like sheepdogs rounded up
a lengthy procession of burning souls,

four abreast, and herded it towards me.
When I might have spit in the fire,
they halted, and Dante, turning on his erstwhile
partner, chivvied him to the head of the
line, then graceful as ivy climbed the abutment
to my side, breathing hard, a
sign of agitation, surely, not
fatigue. Just as a witness in the
box will slowly raise an arm and point to
the accused and say, "He did it" –

the defendant looks away, then gathers
strength and glares right back at him – so

Dante aimed his finger at the blaze he'd
wrangled with, and said, "That one
escaped my notice, incognito, when
I first passed here. Would I have had
the courage to reveal him, I wonder." This,
from one who'd risked death and continued exile
instead of accepting an easy if shameful pardon.
Some moments passed, incinerated.

Canto XXVII

"But things have changed since then. Speak, foulness! I
have brought a representative of
that world your life impoverished. Say the names
that he might know you by, so credit
may be given where credit is due!" Thus Dante.
He replied, "In that dishonored
state of meat and bones your friend remains in,
I was a politician. Like all
politicians, yourself included, my brother in
Christ, I wrote my story large. Of

names, I had both Saul and Paul. The first was
given to me; the second I took.
Which one your friend may recognize, I know not.
He may well be one of the many
who read very little and understand less of the book
I worked so hard to fatten." "Contention's
still your favorite vice, I see, despite
your many teachings of love and compassion.
In my friend's time, there is a vulgar phrase
for men like you: *he needs to get laid.*

But you are not up there with the hypocrites;
although Timothy, reading *Galatians*,
may have wondered why you took his foreskin.
You've sunk like a lead balloon to here.
Now tell my friend what he may thank you for."
Not for the first time, I noticed in Dante a
sarcasm equal (at least!) to my grandfather's own.
The great flame, quivering under its lash,
responded: "You, who peer into this fire
hoping to catch a glimpse of its fuel:

know that when I was in what you in your ignorance
would call *life*, the form I liked to
believe was mine and would be returned to me
some day forever, was short in stature
and balding, not unlike your Wallace Shawn.
That form stood by, approving, the day they
battered my schoolmate Stephen to death. I minded their
coats so their hands would be free. I was not
ready for the faith he'd found. And when I
had that faith burned into me,

I knew that the stones we'd smeared with his blood
expressed my Stephen just as the flesh
we'd torn to smear them expressed him, which is to say,
not at all. And by that token,
you may ruin your eyesight trying to pierce this
double envelope you see here,
blind yourself with curiosity as

I was blinded when faith overcame me,
and nothing essential will have been revealed
you couldn't have learned with your eyes closed."

His tone was affable and mild, but Dante
spoke to him sternly. "Your guilt over Stephen
does not concern us, nor is your radiance such
as will dazzle my friend's sight." I guessed that
Dante was speaking metaphorically; for
certain my physical eyeballs stung and
livid images danced behind my lids.
Said Paul, "You miss my point. There's nothing
for him to see – no flesh, and the spirit is hidden."
Perhaps I was irritated at being

underestimated. To speak gave me pleasure:
"I've read a story or two about you.
You were the apostle to the gentiles. In
Philippi, in Macedonia,
after you had taken over from Barnabas – "
"A good man," that unenlightening
flame interrupted, "but no judge of character."
"– as leader of the mission. Remember?
You encountered a slavegirl. The story goes, a
spirit possessed her. Her owners rented her

out as a sibyl, when the fit was on her.
When she wasn't working, she followed
you and your assistants day after day,

hollering to the streets about you.
She said you served *the supreme god* and that you
brought *a way of salvation*. Did you
have a problem with her message? I can
see you walking along, determined
not to break your stride or hurry, darkly
casting backwards glances. Loony

nuisance one day, maddening drone the next.
The story goes, you couldn't bear it,
turned on her and cast her spirit out."
The flame's tip cocked to the left, like a head
that's thinking, but maybe it was just a breeze.
"I hear that in your time they've found
a way for carnival barkers to preach the gospel.
I wanted only to shut her up.
I learned that power serves desire through excess.
I took her fortune-telling gift

and ruined her, deprived her masters of all
the income she'd brought their family,
and for my pains was deservedly chased from the city,
trailing miracles like bread-crumbs.
But that is not why I have been sent here."
"Had we but world enough and time,"
growled Dante, "we might play your guessing game.
But finer, brighter paths await us.
Spill it now, or I will spill it for you!"
More than once, on an August night,

I have stood on coarse mown grass and watched
emerge from the surrounding woods
a crew of young men and women straining with joyous
abandon to haul a pitchy pine
and toss it on the bonfire. It thuds aslant
and scatters sparks and embers that
the folks with water tanks strapped to their backs, alert
and tense, will quickly extinguish. Then
it settles lower into the pyre, and after
a second when nothing has changed but still

there seems to be a hush, it hugely crackles
and shoots a higher yellow tower
above the bonfire's fiercely snapping banners.
Like that, he swelled and spit words at us,
flinging gouts of syllables skywards at last
I realized were scripture, charring
phrases into memory: *shameful passions,*
in my bodily members a law that
fights against the law my reason approves. Then
with him all his entourage roared

Put to death all the base pursuits of the body
then you will live, and he responded
The fornicator sins against his body,
and they called, *It is a good thing*
for a man to have nothing to do with women.
Then, *Wives, be subject to your husbands!*

in unison they howled, and with call and response
their body-hatred and woman-hatred
crescendoed, climaxed, and subsided to sounds like
applause, or sheets and blankets flapping

on a clothesline in high wind, or the hissing of
man-sized flames. And now I saw the
stunted, desiccated lives that fed them
follow him in procession under our
bridge, and the odor that rose from them was not fragrant.
And it saddened me to observe that
the snake-like line of yellow and blue that cut the
murk as far as I could see
was spotted with many whose self-immolation robed them
in fiery hues of orange and saffron.

Right hand on my shoulder, Dante extended
his left, directing my gaze away
from the mesmerizing flow, and said, "Look there
and you will see the man who sired
the cloud that hung so densely over your childhood,
youth, and even now it towers
behind so much of your sun-struck world – he who,
no less than the head of that serpent passing
below, found his vocation in a blinding
clap of luminosity."

In the distance, in this gently curving
channel cut through the bed of hell,

the blazes blended into a jagged line,
like a photographic negative
of far away trees. Like trees atop a ridge,
where sometimes one, outsized, spikes high,
its middle branches tangled in its neighbors'
tops, so there one flame's tip peaked
above the burning line and nicked the darkness.
"There's your Dr. Edward Teller."

Canto XXVIII

*In my parents' house there was a wall
that was a bookshelf. All the riches
of the world were there, and none forbidden.
After school, before dinner,
I'd spend hours browsing through the titles,
luxuriously savoring.
But there was one that must be hidden whenever
my grandparents came to visit, Shirer's
<u>Rise and Fall of the Third Reich</u>, to spare them
the swastika circled in red on its spine.*

*When I was little I complained to my mom.
Other kids had Christmas. She said,
"But you will always be different, whatever you do.
You can't hide from it, and you can't hide it."
In college, this acquired one of its meanings
the night I sat behind a pillar
in one of the lounges reading Auden unseen by
the jovial group on the other side
and heard arise unchallenged one jovial voice,
"He's not a person, he's a Jew."*

Hesitating, afraid to trust my weight
to this eighth bridge, it sank in through my
eyes there never was a Golden Age.
The Great Mother had jealous sisters.
The People found a new spring and were captured by
the *genius loci*. There was another
way to live. The elders disagreed.
The waters rippled. You could not see
in them your face, your shoulders, arms, or what
you once thought might have been your heart.

Well, we all know how some of us deal with that.
They're here. In his first visit, Dante'd
met a man who'd split a religion in half, the
man who'd counseled Caesar to march on
Rome, a man whose vengeance had cleaved his city
sharply as a diamond but not so
cleanly, a poet whose words had divided a son from his
father to their kingdom's ruin,
and men who for causes now forgotten had
cut themselves off beyond recall.

His words like shockwaves from bombs yet uninvented,
Dante'd reported the waste and ruin.
The souls who'd contributed to society
what splitting mauls give to firewood
he'd watched as they shambled around this sunken ring.
A demon wielding a sword had carved them,
opening gashes and lopping limbs. But yet

the one who trailed his guts had space
to dodder clear of her who blindly stumbled,
dangling her face from the skin of her chin.

Funny how I remember that man's voice,
so young and bland and clear, but can't
recall my high school graduation when
I sat through the pledge of allegiance and
(my father told me) a man behind him said
"I'm glad he's not my son," or even
the nights that year the cops patrolled our street
because some patriotic classmates,
upset by things I'd said about the war,
had patriotically wished me dead.

Those final throes of my teenage years, I railed
against an adult world that wanted,
for reasons obscure but frivolous enough
to lie about, to make me a killer;
but railed with a trust (though constantly disappointed)
in fundamental benevolence
my parents gave me. Others could not share this.
They shipped their faith aboard the Granma,
followed the Yenan Way, dreamed with Che in the
jungle, inhaled old Bolshevik doctrines.

We cried: Ho! Ho! Ho Chi Minh!
N.L.F. is gonna win! and
we cried: Two! Four! Six! Eight!

We don't want a fascist state! and
we cried: Hey! Hey! L.B.J.!
How many kids did you kill today? and
we cried: One! Two! Three! Four!
We don't want your fucking war! and
we cried: Power! Power to the People! and
we cried: The whole world is watching!

In the basement of the University's
Student Union, the sleeping bags
stank rank-sharp of stale tear gas and sweat
among the littered leaflets and banners.
We made fun of the Youth Against War and Fascism
and their clumsy jargon; YAWF
disdained the S.D.S. and they, the hippies;
everyone, the "bourgeois libs."
My mother's warning gained meaning from these things,
in the year Victoria died.

A lion doesn't understand the kind of
prayer where you sit on your tail and feel helpless,
but that is the only kind that most of us offer,
in one or another of its many
variations. How odd it is that we should
become lions when faced with another
face of the thing that sits behind our face.
In such musings I hid myself from
what we had come to and how to get beyond it.
Dante gazed unhelpfully skywards.

"You can't bear to look at it either," I said.
He answered, "I looked to the end of the
Church's temporal power, the concentration
of its energy in one shining
spiritual mass, and Christendom's unification
under the swift and muscular rule of a
monarch wise in this world and divinely tutored.
Instead, this almost amoebic divisiveness,
sectarianism as deadly as dysentery and
mindless, brutal secular states."

Somewhere out there, Dixie's Lost Cause floundered.
(My mother said that Lincoln should have
let them go.) Out there, Ronald Reagan, his
"Contras" and his Mujahideen;
Jinnah, who rode to Partition on a tide of
death; those heroes who squabbled over
the Congo's starving corpse and honored their tribes
by gang-rapes; Mogadishu's vultures;
those true believers who tore the soul out of "comrade" –
all submerged in each other at last.

Overwhelming, the Twentieth Century's proud
perfections of hate: Enver Pasha's
Turks avenging the Ottoman Empire's decline on
their Armenian neighbors; Rwanda's
hand-hewn miracle, eight hundred thousand slain in a
third the time of a baby's gestation! –

an African triumph of the human spirit,
John Henry out-pacing the Nazi machine;
that Holocaust which stands for all the others
and drunkenly shakes its fist at mankind.

Somewhere down there, that demon must have been whirring
like the blade of a Waring Blender.
The trench was filled to the bridge's parapet.
Pressure from the heaving mass
of disarticulated body parts
shifted the walkway's granite slabs
enough that puffs of dust rose from their joints
which clacked as they fell back into place.
The motion, Dante said, was scattered gobbets
trying to pull themselves together.

Canto XXIX

The bridge was not quite yet on the verge of being
swept away, although it shuddered
and strained like an injured animal underfoot.
We hurried, almost running. A quarter
across, I trod down hard on a granite slab
just as the pressure raising it eased,
causing it to thunk into place with more than
usual emphasis. "Hey!" yelled a voice about
twenty feet ahead, off to the right,
"You up there! The one who weighs like a

body that eats! Watch your fucking step!
That was my hip you mashed, jackass!"
I ran and leaned upon the low stone wall and
startlingly near I saw a face
bobbing on the surface, nose skywards,
a white man. "American?" I asked.
The thin lips said, "You bet." "I'm sorry that
I unintentionally caused you pain.
I don't belong in these parts. My guide and I,
we're passing through. We're heading down

and out. If you would like, I'll carry your name
and a message back into living memory."
"Well, you must be a well connected boy.
For what good it might do me, I was
king-maker to the Gipper, taught him how to say
nigger nigger nigger without
offending anyone. I slimed Dukakis
and showed Karl Rove how to drive in the stake.
Tell them, if any of the Holy Rollers
running the GOP will listen,

Lee Atwater says it wa'n't worth it."
I saw the slab begin to shift
again, and when I judged it had reached its height,
I dashed to it and jumped with both feet
on its highest corner. "Hey!" he yelled,
"You little shit, take this then, too:
before the country peeks out from under its shrub,
you'll hear an American audience
applaud a Governor's call to double the number of
concentration camps – and also

cheer a former New York Mayor's endorsement of
torturing captives." He smiled sweetly.
I would have spat on him, but my mouth was dry.
He grinned, and sank much faster than words
could rise to my throat, and when *Oh, land of the free
and home of the brave!* condensed there, his ears
already were deafened deep beneath meat pillows.

"You shouldn't plan on standing there
much longer," said my guide, "unless you think
these stones will float when separated."

So, we walked to solid ground and kept on
walking. I felt as if that whirling
blade behind us had sliced my consciousness in
layers: the top was revulsion at all these
horrors; then was anger at him who led me
through them; then was an infantile
urge to bond with him who led me through them;
then was a deep, deep weariness;
a twinge of anger again; helplessness;
surrender without capitulation;

and darkly at the bottom of the well,
a pool that was still until I dropped in,
that turned out to be tears. I bathed in that darkness
and came out refreshed, to hear my guide
talking. It seemed he was explaining the curious
hodge-podge of light and dark, hot and
cold, that is the infernal environment.
"The common error of those who end here
is to reduce their interconnected, borderless,
mutually dependent world

to an extension of themselves, so this their
theme park reflects their varied tempers,
folded into obdurate landscapes they can

neither accept nor overlook."
Here, the sky was the color of sunlight reflected
in spit on pavement, glossy and glaring.
Behind us, a great dark cloud of birds dropped bodies
into the demonic whirlpool.
Ahead, a rhythmic flicker: blue flashers
beat at the featureless glaze overhead

from atop a shiny, black police car. Stanchions
carried yellow tape across
our path. A chasm opened twenty yards past it.
The squad car door on our side cracked open.
Something like smoke appeared at the top and shoved it wider.
I had thought the windows were tinted,but now they
but now they cleared as darkness poured fomr behind them
smoke-like but denser than smoke, and stood, a six-foot
column, beside the squad car's hooe,
smelling like burnt meat and tappin a nightstick
solidly on a hubcap – *thwack!*

Then its partner got out too, threw two
coils of itself like elbows onto the
roof, and watched. I needed no warning from Dante
to know that here we might have trouble.
He said, "You're a lawyer. Talk to them."
"What's up, officer?" I asked.
"You're the matter, fella. Can't let you pass,
not if you want to keep on pushing
air around." Was that a threat? I asked,

"You mean my friend can go without me?"

"I guess that's up to him." How alone
I felt at merely thinking of it,
how bare on this barren rock, surrounded by phantoms!
For in his presence there was life.
"He's my guide!" "Then I guess you'll stay here, together."
"Why can't we just walk right through?"
We were two on two. Could Dante take them?
The nightstick clunked again. Perhaps
a bruise would join my burns and cuts and welts.
"You can. But I don't think you want to."

"But we have to get through here to get to –
this is willed where what is willed must –"
"Listen to that. Are you listening to that, Bunky?"
"Yup." "*Where what is willed must be!*
They don't make them much like that any more.
You one of those evangelicals, fella?
Nope? Now let me tell you something. You seem
a bit confused. Me and Bunky,
we're kind of like those clowns at the iron gates –
they're not there to keep you out,

they're there because you don't want in. Like us.
We serve and protect, now don't we, Bunky?"
"Oh, yeah." "The boys on the dozers raised us on
the squawkbox, said a live one's coming.
Let me tell you, what we got down there,

no way you want to go through it."
"Why?" "Your weapons designers, your military
engineers, is why, all sitting
at their draughting tables or staring at blank
computer screens in their little cubbies.

Remember how you felt when I told you your friend
could go without you? Sure you do.
Now make that your whole world, and that's a little
what those boys have goin' on.
Man, you get in the middle of all of that, it'll
booglarize you, slow but sure."
So, I asked him if Dante could use his radio,
and while he did, we chatted more.
Perhaps it's some inner punctiliousness; I've always
gotten along well with cops.

He told me, with a name-dropper's pride, of the famous
devisers and builders sunk in that circle:
Archimedes, da Vinci, Teller "with his
teeth in Stanislaw Ulam's skull,"
Alexei Mihailovich Isaev and
Werner von Braun, Kalashnikov and
Colt and Winchester – I don't mind telling you,
my ears got tired. With great relish,
like a man who loves his job, he told me,
"Me and Bunky, we keep them amused.

Don't you never let nobody tell you nothing

happens here. We don't want them
bored, now, Bunky, do we?" "Nope, we don't."
"What we like to do, we like to
come up on them quiet. Bunky does a
great chlorine gas. Show him, Bunky."
Bunky flickered at the edges, the palest
chemical green. "Thank you," I said.
"We do it all. I like the gasses best,
but like the French say, *Shockin' arson*

goop. It's fun to let them set awhile,
then get inside their lungs and make
like anthrax. Unravel hard and fast like shrapnel –
that's a hoot." At last, my friend
set down the bullet-shaped microphone, gave me
a "thumbs up", and rejoined us. Soon,
we heard approaching rapidly from above the
thup thup thup thup thup thup thup thup
that sometimes brings a hail of piercing lead
and this time sang the news of rescue.

Canto XXX

As gently as a mother, having dusted
talc on her baby's bottom, pats it,
Gandhi set the chopper down. The grit the
rotors stirred up stung my cheeks when
Dante, striding erect, led me crouching
out from under. We turned and waved.
Behind us, yellow police tape flapped and snapped in the
wind of Gandhi's leaping departure.
Then it was still. No sound escaped the dun walls
of the cubbies lining the base of the cliff.

From this distance, the cliff looked finger-thick, the
cubbies like pond scum. They were lit sharply
as sometimes happens when weather's breaking and over
there a cloudless patch deluges the
land with glowing, while cloud-shadow bathes us here;
except hell's weather never breaks,
and things are seen there by their own lights.
Where we had landed was tenebrous
as Nagasaki three score years ago
at mid day while the ashes fell.

Before I knew it, we 'd come among the fallen.
Mirror frames as tall as people,
scattered as sparse as the pines on White Rocks Mountain,
leaning so none reflected another,
enclosed their boxes of night in all directions.
I thought at first they were empty, but then,
while I was resting near one, a figure dimly
echoing my posture faded
out of the darkness into the darkness before me.
"Who are you, whose presence calls me?"

•   "He's a pilgrim, and I'm his docent here.
Useless to you, his identity;
but you, sir, may wish him to bring yours back to life,"
Dante hastily answered for me.
"*Sir*, is it? Oh, butter wouldn't melt
in your mouth! That is plain to see."
More shocking than the apparition was the
Boston Irish accent, a blackthorn
smoothed to the New World's uses yet rough enough.
"Now as to your nameless friend, we don't get

many breathing quite so hard come through here.
Looks like he's got his finger on the
pulse or a pulse in his fingers, sure. And he'll be
telling the upper world the news of
me? I think that I will be remembered
through my children, thank you, fine boys
in fine places, fine girls well-placed too.

Not the other way 'round; not them
through me. But you can say you met a man
who knew to a penny the cost of a vote

and that there's not a groat's worth difference
between the living and the dead
when you're stuffing a ballot box, in Southie,
Texas, Illinois, Miami,
or I dare say Brixton or Bangalore.
They all go in feet first and come out
winners. I'll say more: how sweet, to watch your
Tricky Dicks and Loser Als
election eve, to watch them come the statesman
knowing you're holding their short and curlies."

"The *vox pop*. has many mimics," said Dante,
gesturing as if casting a net.
"Sure, and it's a trade that's always needed,
wherever there's government of and for
the people. But that's not all who you might find here,
hidden in the silver, you might say.
There's the throne and the power behind the throne, the
boys I played for and the ones with the
scratch who call the tunes. For sure it's not your
First National Security Trust

Financial Savings Loan and Holding Corp.
that grabs poor sinners by the scruff
and damns them to ever-lasting – but wouldn't you know

they're seeded as thick as a cloud, here, the boys
and girls who'll cobble your name and social numbers
and run up credit as bad as my Aunt
Augusta's elderberry wine. A lot of them,
lately, smelling like piss and plastic.
Ask me another." "Where are the counterfeiters?"
"Moved to another ward, guv'nor.

Had to make room for the card-sharps. Anyways,
who uses cash, these days? Long gone, when
you could line up all the stout-hearted lads you needed
for the price of so many pints of stout!
It's real money now, ain't it, Mr. Diebold?
Ask me another." "Have the perjurers
also been reapportioned – what is the word?"
"Gerrymandered?" I suggested.
"Relocated?" Dante persevered.
"No, you'll find them all about.

Now, don't you be looking around you with those wild eyes,
my anonymous friend, you've not the
strength of vision to see such far-flung sights.
They keep the gas turned low down here.
But if your 'docent' leads you there or there
you'll find a set of matching frames
all in a ring, and facing one another;
the glass in some is curved to make
the belly big, in others a head's a turnip,
a short man's tall, a tall man's squat.

You won't see yourself in them, not even as
others see you. Blown or pinched,
the liars rise to the surface like trout to the fly.
Tell Scooter Libby beware: some day that
Patrick Fitzpatrick will hook him right through the lip.
Now ask me another." "Trapped under glass
in sight of no one – how do you know all this?"
Dante asked what I had wondered.
Again, the hack addressed himself to me.
"Well bless you, my lad, for a good American,

who knows the gerrymander – a Bay State invention,
sure, with the help of that Founding Father and
Tribune of the People Thomas Jefferson.
Still got a free press up there, don't you?
We've our own way here of spreading news.
There's a gang that comes around
once every couple years or so, a horrid
horde, a herd of quacks and shysters.
The lawyers carry the crooked docs in their arms
and over their shoulders and on their backs.

The docs can't walk, you see, being sick with fever
and chills and weeping sores and what all.
They'll stop for a week or two, and then we'll learn
what's doing hereabouts. And then
we're glad to see the back of them, and their snot
and vomit and runny shit all over.

The lawyers are soaked; it makes me bless my fate.
Now ask me another." "No. Time presses.
Come," he said to me, "and leave this wretch with his
schadenfreud, as close to joy as the

laws of this place allow, and not increase it
by lending him ears in which to vent."
I nearly protested that much was still obscure
to me in what he'd said, I'd like
to ask another question and another –
but Dante's hand gently pressed my elbow
and opened a door; behind this door a room;
within this room a space; within,
untiring audience for endless malice,
each of them feeding the other's illusion.

Dazed, I followed him away; had Orpheus
tended his eyes as I did mine, more
children might have been born with his song in their mouths.
Fading behind us, we heard this whine:
"Ask me another… ask me another… please
don't leave so soon… it's silver on one side
and dark on the other and nothing between… for years…
you don't know… punctuated by piss
and snot and puke and shit… you bleedin' guinea,
ask me another… another… please…"

Canto XXXI

"You saw something back there, didn't you?" asked Dante.
"Glimpsed beneath the veil, I mean: the
thing that chases its tail, selfmutilating,
tireless, always a nose behind. That
animal, created in its own image, who
built this place." It didn't seem the
same as what I'd seen, and then it did.
All of a sudden, I wanted to thrust my
arms through seven centuries and hug him.
I tried, and abruptly hugged myself.

This occurred just as I reached the rim to
which he'd led me, clambering up the
inner wall's boulders. An independent observer
might have thought I clutched at him to
pull myself up top, and might have laughed as I
flailed, embraced myself, and tottered.
"Thank you," Dante said mildly, "but I am dead, and
though you'd felt before you came here
how, with a hand on the shoulder, a whispered thought, the
pressure of eyes on the back of the neck, the

dead may touch the living, you also knew the
living never may touch the dead.
Silly boy, so doubting of every truth." And
smiling fondly he tousled my hair.
"Even the ones you have proved to yourself," he added.
The warmth of being seen suffused me.
So we walked and talked of reason's airy
cantilevers, the gulfs faith leaps, the
rope suspended in midair agnostics
traverse, and other beautiful matters.

Cocooned in conversation, I neglected to
wonder how he found his way through the
dull, grey light and mist. Years ago, on
Mount Abe's broad, bald dome, a cloud caught
me and all directions turned to none and
light to a visionless smooth emulsion.
Now it was darker. Yet, eventually,
intermittent hints of form
reminded me that my guide had encountered giants
not far ahead, long ago.

Having visited Monteriggione, I can
attest, as very few others may, that
Dante wrote with precision comparing these
prodigious ambiguities to the
towers clasped in the ring of that hill town's walls,
approached by foot on a foggy night.
Only this, that the slope to them was down,

not up, marred his accuracy.
The evidence of my eyes was so suggestive,
I had to question if I believed it,

because what it suggested was so outrageous.
Like Lot if he'd turned back, or one who
gazes on Medusa, or a tourist
at Mount Rushmore paralyzed with
awe beneath a presidential nostril,
when I was close enough to see him
unobscured by the thick air, I forgot
the way to make my limbs obey me.
He glowed. His uniform was white as snow,
his moustache hairs black as tarred hawsers.

Behind a cliff, his lower half. His bushy
eyebrow might have brushed a third-floor
window's lintel; in the second sub-basement,
his feet. The eyes, dark wading pools,
were small for the broad and blocky face, and swift.
They fastened on us. Can liquid be sharp?
As sharp as the teeth of the things that swam in it
untouched by the light of the lunar crescent
that opened beneath his moustache, a friendly grin,
emitting a crackling, bullhorn voice.

"*Raphèl maì amècche zabì almi!*"
he shouted over and over again.
Dante responded, "O Brilliant Genius

of Mankind! Gardener of
Human Happiness! Great Architect of
Communism! Murderer of
ninety-five thousand priests! But when that other
colossus with facial hair invaded,
then you kneeled to historical necessity
and called to the patriarchs for help!"

Thus commenced a lengthy excoriation
entwined like a trellis of thorny vines
with theopolitical tirades I'd first heard Dante
unleash upon my angry grandfather.
Then, I'd felt excluded. Now, I knew
it all was for my benefit,
this discourse on "social and economic justice
that proceeds only from true religion."
But my mind wandered. Through the thicket of
statistics, the clots of narrative –

"Moscow Trials… dead of famine, millions,
maybe five or six… Great Purge…
Holodomor…" – the ogre shifted, wrenching
my eyeballs. Until now, he'd looked blurry.
I'd thought it was the laden air. Abruptly,
as with the turn of a kaleidoscope's
eyepiece, he came clear. Thousands of tiny,
human forms composed his mass,
an *assemblage* of rococo subtlety
and power, limbs and torsos wrestling,

clenching, leaning, bending, stretching, grasping.
A muscle in his jaw twitched:
committees leaped. He waved his arm: armies
marched. Backs impossibly bent to
hitch his belt. His stomach rumbled: they wept. He
shrugged his shoulders: hundreds slumped with
relief — contortions such as Rodin might have sculpted.
Long after Dante's peroration,
all the silent mile he ushered me
along the circle, they clouded my sight.

We came to another, ranting upon the night.
Luminous monster! The toothbrush moustache
he'd cut back from the full handlebars
that wouldn't fit beneath his gas mask
back in the War To End All Wars (didn't
save him from the British mustard)
rose like a scrap of black forest atop the hill of his
thin-lipped scowl. "Dee *yooo* din!" he howled,
chopping the air with short, forearm strokes.
"Dee *yooo* din!" Dante rushed me forward,

through this oratorical karate.
I crouched and started and stopped and stumbled.
At the cliff's edge, he chucked a rock
I hadn't seen him stoop to grab.
The bellowing stopped. A small, black figure down there
threw its head back; and, above, as

tall as the national tannenbaum, platoons
hauled the cords of the neck to toss that
angry oval visage skywards. The little
biped below us suddenly scrambled

into a cave in the cliff and was gone. Der Fuhrer
disappeared, like flicking a switch. We
gazed down forty feet at the circle of lamps, like
floodlights, the frightened little beast had
stood among, that somehow cast a shadow to
frighten all of us smaller than shadows.
"Would it had been that easy," I said, cheeks hot.
"Should I have let him stay?" asked Dante.
I said, "I don't know. What would I have done?
Spit on him? Or screamed at him?

Knowing I couldn't touch him any more
than I could have in life? This bottomless jug
of hurt he gave me to carry. It can't be emptied."
I gazed down the precipice.
Bitterness, grief and hatred spat in my heart.
I wanted something to melt. I wanted
something molten to pour from me on him, and
hurt him, harden on him, holding him
like a fossil in obsidian, ancient and
sterile. The self likes the sense it has

such powers and durability. But he
was at once too small and too large and too real,

this man whose birthplace I could find on a map,
lay a finger on, pronounce
its name while sweeping with the same hand's fingers
all those places whose names winked out
because he wanted them to be forgotten,
a darkened constellation, home
to people whose blood I carry, who carried those names
into the nameless to join the lost.

"Are we going to see the Chairman?" I asked.
"Mao? It's too far around
to him, and for what? Mere voyeurism – another
monstrous agglomeration like these.
Not much further, we'll find the new way down.
There! Don't you see it? Peeking over the
ledge? Right by that sign. Can you read it?"
COMING SOON TO THIS SITE in black block
letters on a yellow rectangle, then
italics, *YOUR TAX DOLLARS AT WORK,* and

signed, in smaller script, The Management.
I'd thought it was an outcrop of granite, but
now I saw it was someone's grey-haired forehead
just beyond the drop-off. The cliff was
short of the others' navels, but here I could level
my eyes through a part in the hair. *A lesser
monster?* I wondered. *Well-coifed, and strangely immobile.*
Looking over the brink, I beheld
a triple figured totem. On the bottom,

standing stout and square, his features

crammed in the lower part of his face as if
displaced by the out-thrusting force of the great, bald
dome that finished him, Karl Rove; and seated
on his shoulders, clutching a beer can
in one hand, a bird gun in the other,
Cheney; squatting on him, their boss, who
squinted at my feet – all cardboard cutouts
nailed to a sturdy frame. We leaped to the
scaffold, shinnied down the shivering timbers, and
rested in hell's lowest foundation.

Canto XXXII

We stepped off the flagstones abutting the cliff's base,
    onto the stuff that plugs the neck of
    hell's funnel. In his report, Dante had
pleaded for help from the Muses, for language
harsh and rasping enough to say what he found there.
    But I am a child of the Twentieth Century:
Caliban's profit tastes sweet on my tongue. I don't need
    any fucking help to talk rough,
thank you. "Bend over and kiss your ass good-bye" was
    what we made of "duck and cover," and

"duck and cover" was what the people hired by
    mommy and daddy made of their job to
    protect us. Their voices slick as ice were ready
    always to tell us how lucky we were to be
    under their protection. Layered thick as
    glaciers, they still insist on it,
eroding the words: "duh-mocker-sea" and "nashnl
    sskurrity" and "nukkya-ler."
As smooth as a sanded floor, the discourse of liars,
    as slippery as the ice we walked on.

Or maybe it wasn't ice. Perhaps it was
that glass or plastic you see in museum
displays – "Neanderthal Family Cleaning Fish" –
five fur-clad figurines, a pile
of silvery oblongs, posed by a blue-black blob
that borders their snowy clearing : the pond,
polymer aping solidified water. You couldn't
trust your footing on it, though, and
soon we fell into a shuffle and every
unevenness grated the length of my sole.

And it was cold enough to make an ache.
This was the circle of Caïna,
where the heads of the traitors to family stick up
through the – ice? – as silent as cabbages.
Do you want to know who I saw ? My feet passed
right through them, like saws through dreams.
I know because I walked straight through, and all I
saw was the shabby wooden panel
walls of Cameron Brown's puke yellow basement
circa nineteen sixty two.

My brother's friend. By stratagems now forgotten,
the seven-year-olds had prevailed upon
my lordly ten-year-old self to join them downstairs,
where I was to witness marvels.
I didn't want to be there. I was bored.
The promised marvels proved to be toys
that had lost my interest a third of my life ago.

The friends' enthusiasm declined
to squabbling animosity. My brother,
as usual those days, seemed the offender.

I told them so. I washed my hands of it
and took my leave. A minute later,
halfway home, my brother passed me, grimacing,
red-cheeked. I arrived at a scene
of accusation. My father holding court
ex parte disturbed my sense of fairness.
I spoke up for the absent Cameron. Eyes
as calm as a clear sky, hard as hailstones
pierced me. "Even when you think he's wrong,
you must always stand by your brother."

"Your shame becomes you, but it's incommensurable
with the guilt that resides here.
No one's life, my son, was dammed or drained.
You peed in the pond," Dante declaimed
when I told him this story, "like many a swimmer. But here
lie the children of Shiva, destroyer of worlds.
Here OJ's search for Nicole's real killer will end.
Here Erik and Lyle Menendez will savor
their inheritance. Here the Red Guards who told on their
parents march in tight formation.

Here the human bonds arterially
severed leak their substance, pooling,
congealing thicker than amber, and trap them like flies.

But loss of perspective is not uncommon,"
he added abruptly. "Don't let it get you down."
His change of tone brought me fully back
to the miserable present just as my right foot cleanly
bisected ear to ear a head that
closed behind it like water. Its tears, that shattered
on my toes, stung me sharply.

"It's freezing after all," I said. "It's colder
the farther we go," my guide replied.
"Hey!" I said, and stopped. "Didn't you kick and
hit one of these guys, and pull the
hair from his head, when you were... well, like me?
But you said the living can't touch the dead!"
He halted and lifted an eyebrow at me. "I said
the living? You, my vivid friend,
are whom I meant. Or do you believe that you
can lay your flesh by force of will

upon those gone beyond your certainty
that we exist? Of course not! You've
the strength, perhaps, but not the agility. Earthbound,
your place and people. But let's not waste our
time debating whether you wear mind-forg'd
manacles or I was deluded,
unable either of us to prove his point.
Such talk ends only in betraying
our greater brotherhood, one way or another.
I mean *betrayal* in both its senses."

Sometimes, talking to him was like doing a jig saw
puzzle with too many pieces and not enough
edges. *Your people* – was that a medieval Catholic
anti-semitic canard, at last?
He probably meant something else, I thought, but what?
And where did that Janus-faced pun mean to point me?
What brotherhood did we share from which I was also
excluded, like Groucho, who wouldn't belong
to any club that would have him for a member?
And something in his eyes – a need?

Impossible! – called me to hug him. I did, and didn't
care that his mortal part was absent.
"You Americans. Hug and make everything better,"
he smiled, and I knew that was all the answer
I was going to get. Just then, a voice
broke in. It reminded me of a
midwinter morning thirty years ago,
so cold the snow squeaked under my boots.
I'd laid a shovelful of woodstove embers
under my car's oil pan, to warm it.

The starter had turned over with great hesitance.
Just so, this voice cranked itself up.
"Ame…ricans…Ame…ricans…is
that you…Greenglass, at…last, you bastard?"
It might have come from any of those lumps
that studded the murk. Whispering, we

agreed it was near and downwards. Ssh! Ssh!
We slid our feet in the direction
our ears had marked. "Are they…bringing you now,
mein Dovidl? Will you…soon be here?

How will they plant you…I wonder? You won't splash down,
not like me, and melt a hole for
yourself with the heat of your entry, not you, little
sad sack, will you? No, they'll drag you
all the way and maybe then they'll use you
like a jackhammer – that would be right –
to pound yourself a socket. And then we can talk –
you'll talk!" Triangulating on the
increasingly animated vehemence,
we soon stood over its source.

Canto XXXIII

The stuff he was sunk in had gelled around him in ripples
that formed in bas-relief a woman's
face staring up at his chin. His ice-blinded eyes faced
skywards. Upon her forehead, a wisp like a
curl of morning mist on a frozen pond or the
steam from a campfire that's just been doused.
The skin on his sunken temples was black and crinkled.
"It's too quiet," said the man, "If
you were Davie, you would be urging on me the
thing I know: you did it for Ruth."

I looked to Dante. He nodded. "I'm not your Dave.
I'm just a traveler, passing through.
I've miles to go before I sleep." "So that's why
you smell of life," he said. And I:
"One purpose of my wayfaring is to carry
intelligence home from afar. I'd take
great pleasure in delivering any message
you might have – for your friend David,
perhaps? For him to mull on his way here,
Julius, if that is who you are."

"If only Cohn had asked so nicely! What
to say to the living, to prepare
them for their welcome…" "Tell me what he doesn't
know you know." "What you don't know,
you mean! He'd tell you the rest. All right. May his
ears burn! But first, who is your friend?"
"My guide was a fighter for justice – Italian. An exile."
"But not a Jew ? Who knows exile
like the Jews? The Palestinians, maybe.
Tibetans. More and more, Iraqis.

How long are you going to let the masters
of the almighty dollar scare you with
weapons of mass destruction? I was born to the
tired poor and huddled masses
yearning for more than the bosses would ever give them.
I must sound bitter, but these are facts.
That sweet girl Emma Lazarus may have meant every
word, but capitalism makes
freedom and justice a fraud even if they're engraved on a
plaque on a statue in New York harbor, as

all the wretched refuse who washed ashore on the
Lower East Side like my parents found out.
I was seventeen when I met my Ethel,
passionate for a better world,
the year of the Dust Bowl and the CIO.
That year I helped rip the swastika off the
German liner *Bremen* when she anchored in

New York harbor, with Lady Liberty
looking on, and the bliss of living filled me.
The capitalists gave me a free education

in a trade they thought might be useful to them.
I used that time to organize.
Her baby brother David sat at my feet.
I taught him how to fall in step
with the march of time. We three were quite the trio.
He was an idiot, good with his hands.
I was the head, and Ethel, my Ethel, the heart.
I couldn't find a place for Ruth,
his sweetheart, his wife. My downfall was I couldn't
find a way to use her jealousy.

You know, there's a seminar room at my alma mater
named for Colin Powell, who
betrayed almost everything he stood for, in
the name of loyalty. So I
have no regrets for agreeing, on Labor Day
in the year that began with the Wannsee Conference
and ended at the Battle of Stalingrad,
to help our struggling Russian allies.
Stalin may have loved the Jews no more than
Roosevelt did, but he was on the

side of history and the workers and peasants.
So I gave them thousands of helpful
pages, and I gave them a working model

of a proximity fuse they later
used to shoot down spy planes, and I gave them the
idiot, David, the first-class machinist the
army assigned to the labs at Los Alamos. He didn't
realize what Los Alamos was.
But I did, and so did my friends. They called it ENORMOZ.
Ruth helped recruit him. For that, she was useful.

We moved her there to be near him, for running
back and forth, to keep her busy.
He gave us a sketch a six year old might have drawn,
and even for this my friends were grateful.
So my little band of partisans stayed
happy through the long war years.
Did I say happy? No, not that. But useful
solidarity in a good cause
made the suffering and deaths more bearable.
And we had our moments of triumph, my

fuse and Davie's little sketch, for example,
though I could bear no celebrations.
A glass of wine would demean the blood of the fallen.
David, however, took their money.
I told them I would give my right hand to be
chopped if he should let us down.
I was so drunk with belief. After the war, his
brother Bernie, he and I went
into business together, a machine shop.
He was the great machinist, who'd worked on

secrets for the army, after all.
Although I brought what clients we had,
I think he saw me diminished by the peacetime.
I think he thought I'd promised him
that once the Nazi beast was killed the workers'
sun would rise upon Manhattan.
Well, it didn't happen. And our friends
became afraid to use me, except
a time or two on minor missions, and then
his Ruthie resented my 'vacation,'

as if there were more work than David could handle!
She and Bernie called me 'King Tut'
behind my back. So maybe that is why
he told the agents all he knew,
when they came for him. Tell him I know that
it is true: he did it for Ruth,
the one who always stood outside our triangle.
Because she knew she could not have him
wholly unless his sister and I were chopped off,
both of us. She was ruthless,

ha ha! If you can't cry, you have to laugh.
He told them nothing about Ethel.
There was nothing he could tell. But Ruthie
dropped the hint that Ethel typed up
Davie's *verkakte* handwritten notes for our friends.
Then he had to make his choice.

He made it. Not the sister, wife of the fallen
hero, no; the strong one, *his* wife.
I tell you this so he will know I knew.
For him they could name a seminar room.

He had to side with Ruth or call her a liar.
I was a goner already. Ethel?
If he'd told the truth, there was nothing to tell,
and she and he and Ruthie could
have grown old together on memories of me.
What a marriage they'd have then.
I tell you this so she will know I knew,
the family man, the noble protector,
her pawn, her winnings. Ethel, my poor lost queen.
Saypol and Cohn, the prosecutors,

threatened her with death to make her talk,
the dolts, as if no Jewish husband
ever kept his business from his wife.
Not that my Ethel would have talked.
Kaufman, the judge, that idiot, carried through
their threats as if my fuse – and David's
artwork – caused Korea to go up in flames.
May they grow like onions. Speaking of which,
I hear that Cohn is dodging flakes of fire
upstairs. Can you tell me? Is it true?"

I answered, "I have heard that rumor. Although
I'd be much pleased if I could inform

on that career Red-baiter, McCarthy's henchman,
I'd rather enlighten you this way." A soccer-style
kick from the back of his head to the front dislodged
the ice caps from his eyes. They tinkled
among the ridges that curled into Ethel's likeness.
"While you're waiting for your symposium
to convene, enjoy the view," I added,
and we left him with his dead.

Canto XXXIV

So – the world is a very shallow bowl
half filled with drifting obscurities,
and there is a place that is downhill from all of them.
We approached it with footsteps as slow and
deliberate as polar explorers. Scott
was on my mind as much as Amundsen,
which is to say not at all. I'd passed the point
where one puts one foot before the other
for any reason other than that one can
and it would be a betrayal not to.

The surface below us glistened clear and steel-hard.
Probably bodies were buried in it.
I don't remember. I almost bumped into a tractor
parked on the waste and coated with frost. Then,
pointing down the nearly level slope,
Dante said, "There! The center of evil!"
Half a dozen quonset huts, their white paint
dingy, battered by age and use were
set in a haphazard, uneven hexagon
around an immensely tall spire or silo.

Oh, it had grown colder, mile by mile.
The mists looked solid as baseball bats
and water crystals that glinted, did so piercingly.
Breath plumed out of my nostrils in ropes.
Above a door at the silo's base, a sign:
"Satan – 9:00 to 5:00 Weekdays/
Closed On *Shabbos* Sundays Legal Holidays."
On the stoop, a basket held a
handlettered placard: "HONOR SYSTEM/please/
contribute whatever you think is right."

The door bore a huge, rusty padlock. Dante
shook the basket, put it back.
"No key. Nothing." Repressing a shiver, I pointed
to another sign that directed
"Visitors Register At Administration."
(Yes, the signs' black alphabet
spelled English, to my eyes.) But, what way?
The choices were few enough. The sixth
we tried, the doorknob twisted freely, swinging
into a well-lit, spacious room.

The door's springs slammed it shut behind us. Warmth,
having struggled from a pot-bellied stove
in the farthest corner, embraced me feebly. I stood
as still as if impeded by welcoming
arms flung fondly about my neck. And thus, the
penultimate temptation ensnared me:
to grow so accustomed to hell as to accept

what solace for its ills it offers.
With lethargic detachment, I watched Dante
stride around the phalanx of empty

chairs that occupied most of the room, to a window
in the wall across from the entrance.
There he stopped and turned to his left, apparently
thinking I'd followed. His angry glare and
brusque gesture made me hurry to join him.
It was like the jolt of a winch.
Not the way you'd think, that his attraction
pulled me – rather, a motor lurched
awake within me, reeling me to his anchor.
Behind the window, a moon-faced woman

uniformed in navy blue smiled thinly.
"Please to take a number," she said,
and shoved two chits through a slot in the window glass.
Dante picked them off the counter and
handed one to me. She pointed up at a
box above the window, in which
red digits glowed – 134.
Dante's chit read 98, mine
483. "Please wait until you're called,"
the woman said, her smile unceasing.

"Could you say how long that might be?" I asked.
Again she pointed, with a gesture
eerily reminiscent of the Baptist's

in the painting by Leonardo.
"We are waiting to serve one-thirty-four.
Then we will serve one-thirty-five.
You may pass the time by watching our welcome
slide show in the auditorium.
Very informative. Many say they like it."
She lowered her forearm clockwise until

her forefinger (that in Leonardo's picture
beckons and commands) halted
horizontally at three o'clock, still
smiling vacantly. I stared
until my guide said, "She must mean for us to
enter there," and walked to an unmarked
door to the right of the window and turned the knob.
It led to a small, narrow room,
a few ranks of weary-bottomed theatre seats,
a rippled, speckled screen. We sat.

The lights dimmed. I found the narration hard to follow,
the sound jumped so, from the tinny blur
of a high school public address, to cinematic
clarity, to the bludgeoning shock of
bullhorns, to the crackle and blare loudspeakers
pour on concentration camps,
prison yards, and subjugated cities.
The pictures were grainy, their colors faded.
"Measuring eight hundred seventeen feet from crown to
toe/three heads/six arms/and wings that

generated the thrust of/several Boeing
747s,/the Prince of
Darkness, Father of Lies, Beelzebub,
Lucifer, Sheitan/former first
among the angels/today is preserved where he fell
in this magnificent structure that pierces
the sky/from the center of his kingdom/modeled
upon the humble agricultural/
and military storage facilities/that
dot America's heartland/reminding

awestruck visitors/that the seeds of the past are
missiles aimed at the future/his lordship..."
Dante quietly sat beside me, his hands
folded in his lap, his head
thrown back. Was that a snore? It was! It shocked me
more than anything had so far.
I felt he'd abandoned me to the moon-faced lady.
My rock, my goad, my comfort, dissolved.
I sat with that awhile. Here, in the cheap seats,
watching the only show in town,

I learned at last that this place lays claim to us all
because we are born desirous and ignorant
beyond renunciation or denial.
Abandon hope, ye who enter.
Had I believed by burning my draft card I'd end
the war; by writing letters I'd change

the government; by smoking dope I'd cure
all pain; by freely making love
I'd set love free? I smiled. *Non serviam.*
I knew the thing that I could do.

Perhaps Dante sensed my shoulders untensing.
He leaned to me and said, as clear
as an usher's flashlight's beam, "Yes. It's time."
We rose, as silent and easy as smoke
whose nature it is to rise, and walked to the exit
and out past the chairs. Now I saw
the skeletons slumping in them – and was one mine?
The door's springs loudly protested, opening.
Frigid air rushed in and slapped my body.
I listened. No sound from behind.

At the base of the monstrous, smooth-skinned shaft,
I thought of the Sackler Museum's lingam,
carved from a single crystal, tall as a man.
I asked if Dante knew of it.
He said, "That rosy quartz is a greater danger
to your country than any warhead.
Its vibrations flood your capitol, driving
unsuspecting leaders mad.
They should send it back to those with knowledge
how to worship and control it."

You in the District who worship and control
so very few things, there's your warning!

Nearby, the sign that said go to Administration.
I flung myself upon it, buffeted it
front and back until the frozen grip of the
ground was loosened. Then I yanked it
upwards inch by heaving inch. At last, with
bloody hands, I held five feet of
metal pole. When my breathing slowed, I
swung it hard at the silo's padlock,

trusting in hell to have used something cheap and flimsy.
My faith was vindicated: after
half a dozen blows, the shackle broke.
Floodlamps harshly lit the inside.
A plaque by the door said , "You are within a cylinder
taller than St. Peter's dome by
nineteen yards." Looking up it, vertigo
almost made me swoon. I dropped my
gaze. It fell upon a souvenir stand,
not much larger than the carts that

surround the Mall in Washington, parked by the wall
to our right. "Something For Everybody"
proclaimed its awning. Its shelves were piled with lanyards,
dolls and oven mitts woven from coarse, dark
"Satan's hair fiber 100%" (I swiped one).
You could have your name embroidered
with it on a bill cap, t-shirt, sweatshirt,
hoodie, scarf, or priestly vestment.
Nobody tended the stall. The only echoes

were our own. "We'd better hurry

before Security comes," said Dante, walking
towards the center, where there was nothing,
no trapped Lucifer long as an aircraft carrier's
flight deck, just a hole in the floor
emitting the faintest whiff of sulphur, and also
a hint of the sweetness of new-mown hay.
He paused at the brink, and held his hand to me,
a pace behind, and let me feel his
fingers entwine with mine. One breath left me.
Then we stepped into the void.

Afterword, With A Note On Notes

At last I got tired of trying to explain to my friends just what it was that I saw in Dante's *Comedy*. It might have appeared to them as a harmless obsession, differing from others in which I periodically indulged – fly fishing, the novels of Henry James and Patrick O'Brien, certain television series – mainly in that it never went away. Once very year or so I would read through from the first line of the *Inferno* to the last of *Paradiso*. How to explain the attraction of a late medieval Catholic vision of the afterlife, however exalted its reputation, for a very contemporary agnostic-Jewish-Buddhist American?

Usually, my attempts at describing the multi-dimensional vivacity of the work ended up as lists of various qualities: psychological acuteness, vivid sensory imagery, powerful spirituality, wicked humor, exciting plot (at least in the *Inferno*), intellectual rigor, commitment to social justice, stunning architectonic force and intricacy, muscular language, driving prosody, etc. etc. blah blah blah. Or I might try to focus on one aspect as a way to enter all the others, for example, that it is a buddy story focused (for its first two-thirds) on the relationship between a perceptive, emotionally volatile, erring but well-meaning Dante and his rather strict and demanding but not entirely unplayful mentor; a love story, centered on a great romance that is requited only after years and trials, and in ways that neither principal could have anticipated; a guru story; a philosophical/theological novel in verse form; a tale of mid-life crisis; a road adventure seven hundred years before Kerouac; a sci-fi extravaganza so special in its effects that they'll never be able to film it successfully. Every time, no matter what my strategy, the explanation petered out, communicating at most that this is a strange mishmash which contains reasons why a person might become obsessed with it ... but, still!

No matter how thoroughly I might explicate the poem's many allusions and obscurities, no matter how deftly I might analyze its components and structure, the essence of the thing lies far beyond those. I have a notion that, like dreams, all poetry is ultimately about its author. More than any other work of which I am aware, Dante's *Comedy* presents an entire human being in all his fullness, and a brilliant, infuriating, hilarious, passionate, perceptive, insightful, subtle, dunder-headed, joyous, compassionate, complex person he is. But there I go again, with the lists. To say Dante lives in his poem, almost seven hundred years after his death, sounds like hyperbole and invites misunderstanding. But he is there. I have met him. The encounter with him is overwhelming.

At some point I realized that the only way to capture and communicate all the dimensions, every level of my experience, would be to write directly about it. I can describe baseball to you by telling you about all its rules, its history, its equipment, its personalities, its literature, its fandom. Or I can tell you what it's like to play the game. The former method may educate you about baseball, but the latter will put you inside it. So I undertook to rewrite the *Comedy* as if it happened to me; not as a translation,[1] or as an adaptation, but as my own experience.

This was not a matter of mere substitution (e.g., the wicked politicians of my time for the wicked politicians of his), although there certainly is fun to be had in that exercise. *Plus ça change, plus c'est la même chose.* But that is the most trivial of games. Although his Italian speaks clearly of things that I recognize on Vermont's streets every day, what a different cosmos he inhabited. How alien might we find each other? How mutually incomprehensible! How fascinating to seek the deeper empathy that comprehends the things in his cosmos for which I have no counterpart. How frightening and rewarding to know that there are irreconcilable differences between us concerning matters of the gravest importance that do not disrupt but rather feed the creative tension which is our bond.

It took a while to outgrow my humility before Dante's great work and my sense of transgression in approaching it this way, the utter cheek of supposing I could in any sense make it mine. At a fairly early stage I told friends that I felt as if I were building a full-scale model of the Eiffel Tower with toothpicks. Then I stopped worrying about the audaciousness of the task and my fitness for it, and simply allowed myself to be as aware as I could of the polyphonic resonance, the living dialogue with a poet two thirds of a millenium deceased, that I had set myself to record. I hope that readers will accept my work in that spirit and perhaps find through it some points of entry to the place where Dante's world and ours uneasily but lovingly continue to coexist.

I spoke of Dante's allusions and obscurities. I spent years picking my way to Dante through dense encrustations of footnotes. Any modern reader not already a scholar of the late Middle Ages in Tuscany must do so. I am envious of those who read Dante early, before there was need of explication of the names of prominent Ghibelline families and the like. It is, to adopt another metaphor, the difference between having him burst upon one undimmed and, on the other hand, watching him slowly rise to meet one out of great depths, his shine gradually increasing until there he is before one, in need of polishing. Well, his effulgence will bear it. I am afraid that mine won't. I have therefore eschewed footnotes, and I have tried to keep my allusions to the bare minimum required of a poem which must necessarily be allusive, and always to provide enough context so that the reader need not become too frustrated. Some obscurity is unavoidable, if only because knowledge has become so atomized that two people, both thoroughly educated, may have very few points of reference in common. Not every reader who knows, for example, that the nickname of former House Majority Leader Tom DeLay was "The Hammer" will also know that the apostle Paul, who subjected his disciple Timothy to circumcision in order to facilitate their mission, argued in *Galatians* against the necessity of gentiles' observing that ritual. The desperate may resort to Wikipedia.

---

[1] For that, I cannot imagine better than the one by Robert and Jean Hollander, which has become my constant companion and guide.

Fomite

About Fomite

A fomite is a medium capable of transmitting infectious organisms from one individual to another.

"The activity of art is based on the capacity of people to be infected by the feelings of others." Tolstoy, *What Is Art?*

Writing a review on Amazon, Good Reads, Shelfari, Library Thing or other social media sites for readers will help the progress of independent publishing. To submit a review, go to the book page on any of the sites and follow the links for reviews. Books from independent presses rely on reader to reader communications.

For more information or to order any of our books, visit
http://www.fomitepress.com/FOMITE/Our_Books.html

More Titles from Fomite...

Novels
Joshua Amses — *During This, Our Nadir*
Joshua Amses — *Raven or Crow*
Joshua Amses — *The Moment Before an Injury*
Jaysinh Birjepatel — *The Good Muslim of Jackson Heights*
Jaysinh Birjepatel — *Nothing Beside Remains*
David Brizer — *Victor Rand*
Paula Closson Buck — *Summer on the Cold War Planet*
Marc Estrin — *Hyde*
Marc Estrin — *Speckled Vanitie*
Zdravka Evtimova — *Sinfonia Bulgarica*
Daniel Forbes — *Derail This Train Wreck*
Greg Guma — *Dons of Time*
Richard Hawley — *The Three Lives of Jonathan Force*
Lamar Herrin — *Father Figure*
Ron Jacobs — *All the Sinners Saints*

Ron Jacobs — *Short Order Frame Up*
Ron Jacobs — *The Co-conspirator's Tale*
Scott Archer Jones — *A Rising Tide of People Swept Away*
Maggie Kast — *A Free Unsullied Land*
Darrell Kastin — *Shadowboxing with Bukowski*
Coleen Kearon — *Feminist on Fire*
Jan Englis Leary — *Thicker Than Blood*
Diane Lefer — *Confessions of a Carnivore*
Rob Lenihan — *Born Speaking Lies*
Ilan Mochari — *Zinsky the Obscure*
Gregory Papadoyiannis — *The Baby Jazz*
Andy Potok — *My Father's Keeper*
Robert Rosenberg — *Isles of the Blind*
Fred Skolnik — *Rafi's World*
Lynn Sloan — *Principles of Navigation*
L.E. Smith — *The Consequence of Gesture*
L.E. Smith — *Travers' Inferno*
Bob Sommer — *A Great Fullness*
Tom Walker — *A Day in the Life*
Susan V. Weiss — *My God, What Have We Done?*
Peter M. Wheelwright — *As It Is On Earth*
Suzie Wizowaty — *The Return of Jason Green*

Poetry
Antonello Borra — *Alfabestiario*
Antonello Borra — *AlphaBetaBestiaro*
James Connolly — *Picking Up the Bodies*
Greg Delanty — *Loosestrife*
Mason Drukman — *Drawing on Life*
J. C. Ellefson — *Foreign Tales of Exemplum and Woe*
Anna Faktorovich — *Improvisational Arguments*
Barry Goldensohn — *Snake in the Spine, Wolf in the Heart*
Barry Goldensohn — *The Hundred Yard Dash Man*
Barry Goldensohn — *The Listener Aspires to the Condition of Music*
R. L. Green When — *You Remember Deir Yassin*
Kate Magill — *Roadworthy Creature, Roadworthy Craft*

Tony Magistrale — *Entanglements*
Sherry Olson — *Four-Way Stop*
Janice Miller Potter — *Meanwell*
Joseph D. Reich — *Connecting the Dots to Shangrila*
Joseph D. Reich — *The Hole That Runs Through Utopia*
Joseph D. Reich — *The Housing Market*
Joseph D. Reich — *The Derivation of Cowboys and Indians*
David Schein — *My Murder and Other Local News*
Scott T. Starbuck — *Industrial Oz*
Seth Steinzor — *Among the Lost*
Seth Steinzor — *To Join the Lost*
Susan Thomas — *The Empty Notebook Interrogates Itself*
Sharon Webster — *Everyone Lives Here*
Tony Whedon — *The Tres Riches Heures*
Tony Whedon — *The Falkland Quartet*

Stories
Jay Boyer — *Flight*
Michael Cocchiarale — *Still Time*
Neil Connelly — *In the Wake of Our Vows*
Catherine Zobal Dent — *Unfinished Stories of Girls*
Zdravka Evtimova — *Carts and Other Stories*
John Michael Flynn — *Off to the Next Wherever*
Elizabeth Genovise — *Where There Are Two or More*
Andrei Guriuanu — *Body of Work*
Derek Furr — *Semitones*
Derek Furr — *Suite for Three Voices*
Zeke Jarvis — *In A Family Way*
Marjorie Maddox — *What She Was Saying*
William Marquess — *Boom-shacka-lacka*
Gary Miller — *Museum of the Americas*
Jennifer Anne Moses — *Visiting Hours*
Martin Ott — *Interrogations*
Jack Pulaski — *Love's Labours*
Charles Rafferty — *Saturday Night at Magellan's*
Kathryn Roberts — *Companion Plants*

Ron Savage — *What We Do For Love*
L.E. Smith — *Views Cost Extra*
Susan Thomas — *Among Angelic Orders*
Tom Walker — *Signed Confessions*
Silas Dent Zobal — *The Inconvenience of the Wings*

Odd Birds
Micheal Breiner — *the way none of this happened*
David Ross Gunn — *Cautionary Chronicles*
Gail Holst-Warhaft — *The Fall of Athens*
Roger Leboitz — *A Guide to the Western Slopes and the Outlying Area*
dug Nap— *Artsy Fartsy*
Delia Bell Robinson — *A Shirtwaist Story*
Peter Schumann — *Planet Kasper, Volumes One and Two*
Peter Schumann — *Bread & Sentences*
Peter Schumann — *Faust 3*
Peter Schumann — *We*

Plays
Stephen Goldberg — *Screwed and Other Plays*
Michele Markarian — *Unborn Children of America*

www.ingramcontent.com/pod-product-compliance
Lightning Source LLC
Chambersburg PA
CBHW021432080526
44588CB00009B/509